C.H.U.R.C.H.
A VISION OF WHAT THE
CHURCH COULD BE

Dennis R. Fakes

iUniverse, Inc.
New York   Bloomington

C.H.U.R.C.H.

A Vision of What the Church Could Be

iUniverse books may be ordered through booksellers or by contacting:

iUniverse

1663 Liberty Drive

Bloomington, IN 47403

www.iuniverse.com

1-800-Authors (1-800-288-4677)

ISBN: 978-0-595-52845-5 (pbk)

ISBN: 978-0-595-62899-5 (ebk)

Printed in the United States of America

ACKNOWLEDGEMENTS

I have many people to thank for this little book. I especially thank the people of St. Mark's Evangelical Lutheran Church, Huntsville, Alabama who are using this book in the fall of 2008 to renew their faith and re-envision the C.H.U.R.C.H. Much of this material began as a sermon series in the Epiphany season of 2007.

My wife Hilda has put up with many lonely hours while I labored to get this manuscript done in time for publication.

The staff at St. Mark's has been a wonderful, inspirational joy. They have been willing to work around me on this project. I thank them!

Unless otherwise noted, all scripture references are from the **New Revised Standard Version Bible,** copyright © 1989 National Council of the Churches of Christ in the United States of America. Used by permission. All rights reserved.

I have also used **THE MESSAGE**, copyright © 1993, 1994, 1995, 1996, 2000, 2001, 2002. Used by permission of NavPress Publishing Group."

July 2, 2008

C.H.U.R.C.H.

This little book is about the church. Or, as one of our members calls it, "the glorious church."

I read an article recently about the worst jobs in the world. Jobs such as: Worm parasitologist, landfill monitor, Iraqi archaeologist, Tick dragger, computer help-desk tech, root sorter and TV meteorologist.

As pastor I have the best job in the world! I have the marvelous privilege and opportunity to help people in that which we human beings want and need most.

What do people want and need?
1. People need a purpose in living.
2. People need to know that life has hope.
3. People need community & intimacy with God, others and themselves.
4. People need uniqueness and individuality—a strong sense of identity.

I believe the church is the one agency in our world today that can answer the deep longings and needs of people.

This is why I say I have the very best job in the world! And ALL OF US have the opportunity to engage in activities that fulfill the deepest needs of people.

Russ Blowers was pastor of East 91st Street Church in Indianapolis, Indiana for forty-six years (1951 - 1996). He went home to the Lord in November of 2007. As a minister he was active in his local Indianapolis Rotary club. At club meetings each week a member gives a brief statement about his job.

When it was his turn, Russ said:

"I'm with a global enterprise. We have branches in every country in the world. We have our representatives in nearly every parliament and board room on earth. We're into motivation and behavior alteration.

"We run hospitals, feeding stations, crisis pregnancy centers, universities, publishing houses, and nursing homes. We care for our clients from birth to death.

"We are into life insurance and fire insurance. We perform spiritual heart transplants. Our original Organizer owns all the real estate on earth plus an assortment of galaxies and constellations. He knows everything and lives everywhere. Our product is free for the asking. (There's not enough money to buy it.)

"Our CEO was born in a hick town, worked as a carpenter, didn't own a home, was misunderstood by his family, hated by enemies, walked on water, was condemned to death without a trial, and arose from the dead--I talk with him everyday."

Russ Blowers was of a generation that loved and trusted organizations. He found in the church the most amazing organization in the world! But it is far more than an organization. In fact the church can be far less an *organization* and more a *movement*. This distinction, as we will see, makes quite a difference.

Like so many people, I have a distrust of organizations. On the surface, the church looks like a typical organization. There is a Constitution, By-laws, Continuing Resolutions, etc. There are Annual Meetings, elections, budgets—all those things that *organizations* have (but, interestingly, would have been quite foreign to Jesus and the disciples).

This organizational nature of the church is necessitated on several fronts. The first is the human desire to organize and make sense of groupings of people. The other reason for excessive organization is to protect the church from legal entanglements. A third, and hopefully least important function of organization, is control. The checks and balances feature of the American Constitution works so well that we immediately translate that feature into any larger grouping of people. Tyrants can rule churches as they can nations. A controlled organization can more likely prevent that from happening.

But try to shift your thinking away from the idea of church as *organization* and to the idea of the church as a *movement.* Movements are transitory. Movements change people in significant ways. Movements are historical. It is hard sometimes to get one's hands around a movement. Yet, I am convinced, the church is at its best when it is more a *movement* and less an *organization.*

So--what is the church? Or, as I spell it here: C.H.U.R.C.H.

C = CHRIST

It all begins and ends with a person: CHRIST. Here in this one person, we receive our meaning and purpose for life and living. Each Christian is called to live in relationship with Jesus Christ.

That relationship often begins even before conscious awareness of relationships. It often begins in Baptism: in this holy sacrament, we receive our IDENTITY ("Christening") as a UNIQUE & CALLED individual.

In Christ we find community with others who are also part of the body of Christ. In the Holy Communion (the word coming from the word "community"), we receive bread and wine that becomes incorporated into our individual bodies as we corporately live out our calling and ministry as Christ's presence in this world. Jesus says, **"Very truly, I tell you, the one who believes in me will also do the works that I do and, in fact, will do greater works than these, because I am going to the Father."** (John 14:12)

As Christ's sacred body, the C.H.U.R.C.H., we will do greater works than even he!

Think of it. Every day, millions are fed in the name of Christ. Every day around the world, millions are healed in the name of Christ. Every day—especially on Sunday's—God's word is proclaimed to millions—not just thousands.

In Christ we find intimacy with God—the barriers came down when Christ came down from the cross. When the temple curtain was torn on Good Friday, all believers in Christ gained immediate access to the Holy of Holies. Jesus, our great High Priest, made each of us to be priests.

In Christ we know we have hope. The beautiful passages of John 11 or 14 or Romans 8—passages usually read at funerals—proclaim the amazing hope that Christ has indeed defeated our great nemesis death and the grave.

And our hope is not just for the world to come but it surfaces every day in the life of the Christian because we know, as the old children's song says, "He's got the whole world in his hands."

In Christ is everything human beings need beyond, air, food and shelter.

H = HOME

Home is where we belong. Everyone needs to belong somewhere. It's more than a physical PLACE—it's the place of the heart. Home is where we love and are loved. It is (hopefully—though not always in the real world) a safe place. It is a place where I can "let my hair down" and just be the joy God has created.

The average person will move fourteen times in a lifetime. Forty percent of us were born in a different state than the one we currently live in. At St. Mark's I'm sure it is even more. I would guess that as many as ninety percent of us were born in a different state.

With people always on the move, the sense of home has gotten lost. Many people feel a real disconnect with their environment because the sense of place has been lost. Yet the church is the one place where people should find a home. And it should be more than a spiritual home.

Home is where we are accepted as we are (unconditional acceptance: GRACE). Most of the world is judging us and we are frequently tempted to judge others. But when the church is at its best we let go of our judgment. We learn the art of acceptance.

The church is our HOME. At the church I served in California, I had a very gifted song writer and musician who created a wonderful piece of music called, "The church is our home; our home is the church…" It was catchy and every time I think of the church as a home, that song replays itself in my brain.

Too often people don't think of the church as a home because, when they think of the church, they think way too small. They think of Sunday morning worship. Many active, life-long church-goers fall into this camp. It is the camp that is related to the idea of the church as an *organization* instead of as a *movement.*

As churches grow in membership one of the things people fear most is the fear of not knowing everyone. In my thirty-five years of being in the church, the fear that "we won't know everybody" has been the great emergency break to fulfilling the Great Commission.

This fear is real and it is true. Studies have shown that the average person can only relate to about 150 people in any real sense of relationship. I am fascinated by studies showing this 150 cap that plays out in all kinds of people gatherings. Very few can relate in a very meaningful way to more than 150 people. Two British scientists, R. A. Hill and R.I.M. Dunbar published an article in "Human Nature" (2003, 14:53-72) entitled "Social Network Size in Humans." What is fascinating to me is that they found that 150 is a fairly accurate number of maximum relationships the average person can handle. Think of your Christmas card list or check out your e-mail list—I would venture a guess that you will find this rule of 150 pretty prevalent in your own life.

In my second church, the congregation was very pastor-oriented. We grew rapidly from an average of thirty-six the year before I arrived to an average attendance of 149 five years later. I didn't have enough sense to see that we had maxed out on pastor-oriented ministry. We needed more staff and we desperately needed small groups. For five years we grew rapidly and then for the next six years we plateaued—all because we did not understand the 150 rule.

For the church to be a home, it has to be such in the small groups we find and NOT in our Sunday morning relationships. This is a real paradigm shift. It means changing our thinking about the church as a home. Those Sunday morning relationships are important, but the barriers of loneliness, alienation, and the walls that isolate only come down in small, intimate, spiritual groups of people. At St. Mark's we call them "L.I.F.E." Groups because at their best they show Love, Intercession (prayer), Fellowship, and Encouragement.

U=URGENCY

How quickly time flies! Human life is incredibly short. I think of this as I look at the limestone hills around Huntsville. Limestone is made of billions upon billions of marine animals from millions of years ago. That these tall hills were once on the bottom of a sea is very humbling. I noticed the same thing growing up in Western Kansas. Our little town was surrounded by limestone hills and on the TOP of these hills you could find the best SEA fossils in the world—mostly clam shells. The fact that this which obviously was once the BOTTOM of a sea is now the TOP of a hill would indicate some natural forces far greater than my limited experience with human years. Human years are short.

Since life is short, there is a natural sense of urgency.

This home we call the "church" is a place of comfort and peace, but it is also a place of URGENCY. The news is true GOOD NEWS— and people don't keep good news to themselves.

Too often churches get caught up in being bad news places. They forget their mission to be bearers of GOOD NEWS and instead become places of judgment, gossip, griping, complaining, pettiness and smallness. (The surest proof of Satan is what one finds in churches— because Satan is always seeking to lead churches and church members to forget the urgent, exciting, wonderful GOOD NEWS they are called to proclaim). Former classmate and Bishop Stephen Bowman shared with us at a recent Synod Assembly that we are "a minority on a mission with a mandate from the Master." Well put!

David Kinnaman, president of the Barna Institute was commissioned to do extensive research on what young Americans think about Christianity. Here is what the research uncovered: Mosaics and Busters (the generations that include late teens to early thirtysomethings) believe Christians are judgmental, anti-homosexual, hypocritical, too political and sheltered.

Many non-Christian or unchurched people see the church as being after their money or seeking to control them in one way or another.

The church has a bad reputation. Some of that reputation is deserved by what passes for Christianity on television, in movies, and books. Too often the church has gotten off track—sometimes WAY off track. There is an urgent need to reaffirm the C.H.U.R.C.H. as a *movement* that meets human need.

I believe that as we live out our purpose as the church—fulfilling human need—we will grow. Every church, like every living entity, is either growing or declining. Retaining homeostasis among living things is impossible. The church may not fare well as an *organization* but as a living *organization* that is growing and thriving. Unfortunately some eighty-five to ninety percent of the churches in America are in decline. Somehow the *organism*, the *movement*, has become petrified as an *organization*.

How have we kept the sense of urgency under wrap and how long will we remain complacent about our mission? When will we let the Master move us into mission?

R = RELATIONSHIPS

The primary purpose of the church is to CONNECT PEOPLE WITH GOD. The church is, bottom-line, a spiritual community. But when most people think of church they do not connect "spirituality" with "church". I've had many people tell me, "I'm a spiritual person but not religious." And, I must confess, I've met many church-goers who are not particularly spiritual. Sometimes I sit through church meetings and the word "God" or "Christ" doesn't even come up. The sense that we are all about connecting people with God does not even seem to be on the radar of many church meetings.

Writing in 1962, the American activist theologian William Stringfellow put it this way:

As I find it, religion in America… has virtually nothing to do with God and has little to do with the practical lives of men in society. Religion seems, mainly, to have to do with religion. (From *The Christian Century*, April 22, 2008)

Every one of us has a God-place within us that needs to be filled. Human beings are spiritual beings. They have a God need. From our earliest ancestors we learn from fossil remains that their spiritual interest was important. In fact, looking at past societies, we can see that the spiritual impulse in human beings has often been huge. Think of the pyramids of Egypt or the ancient temples of Greece and Rome. Look at the majestic cathedrals of Europe. All these august monuments attest to the spiritual impulse in human beings. The greatest of human effort went into spiritual causes.

The church is the one agency, the body that God has chosen to fulfill that function of filling people with God so that hearts can have peace and joy. Saying it again, we are in the business of connecting people with God. God works through the Holy Spirit in the church.

The secondary purpose of the church is to CONNECT PEOPLE WITH ONE ANOTHER. There is definitely a social element to the church.

In earlier times this was more prominent. Stores were closed on Sundays. If you wanted to connect with others, Sunday was the time to do it and church was the place. The work week was so demanding that there wasn't the time necessary for satisfactory relationships. But Sundays were set aside for physical rest. Sundays were set aside for worship and people-mingling.

Today there are many things to do on Sundays. In fact, Sundays are increasingly becoming less distinct as special days. Increasingly Sunday looks like Tuesday or Friday. Perhaps even more, Sundays are becoming busier days than the rest of the week as we seek to cram into that one day all that didn't get done the week just past.

But the human need for connection continues and the isolation people experience has actually increased. We no longer have porches people sit on to keep cool because we've got air-conditioning. Sidewalks are not generally used to connect people and homes. The concept of "family room" has been replaced by "media center." Television, text-messaging, "Facebook", "My Space", and the game box have replaced the face-to-face interactions people need.

These modern times where people become digital numbers, are times that cry out for uniqueness and individuality: Our NAMES are important! We have PERSONALITIES that are special. We have special GIFTS that need developing and utilization.

Many of us feel de-personalized, isolated, cut-off from others. The church can be the answer—especially when the church is about small groups of friends.

C = CALLING

When my daughter was a child, she was identified as "gifted" and was placed on a special "gifted" track at school. I knew she was special. But what I have learned through life experience and reading scripture is that we are ALL special; ALL gifted. How easily we can forget that we are all special because we are ALL gifted. Every one of us is uniquely special. Every individual has talents and abilities, life experiences, and aptitudes not shared with anyone else in the same proportions.

God has created each of us UNIQUE. That is a gift. Too often we see people who are different from us as threats. "She's weird!" "What a jock!" "A Goth!" The church can help people discover their differences and see these differences as gifts and not as threats.

I have found that most people really don't know their own gifts and uniqueness. They don't know how precious their "one-of-a-kind" personality is. We easily understand the special nature of a Rembrandt painting or a Michelangelo sculpture. To own a single piece would be worth millions. Yet we, too, are exceedingly rare and priceless.

Furthermore, our gifts are not ours to hoard and enjoy only for ourselves. We are gifted to serve others and when we use our gifts in this way, life comes alive.

Modern American society does not agree. Most of what I read, see, and understand is that "it is all about me." It's not. It is about me using myself for others.

I've been to Israel on four different occasions. I love the country for its history and relationship to Christianity. But this little country (no larger than the state of New Jersey) is also a geological wonder. The Jordan River begins at the base of Mt. Hermon. It flows south and empties into the beautiful Sea of Galilee. This fresh water lake is filled with life and abundance. At the other side of the sea the Jordan River resumes its course to the Dead Sea. It is called the "Dead" sea because there is no life there. The Dead Sea is a lake that does nothing but receive. It never shares its waters. It only receives them.

What an apt illustration of human life. The person who only receives ends up being a mighty unhealthy entity. But the person who receives AND gives, follows the law of human life.

The church teaches that principle and is constantly asking its members to give of themselves as they have received. Again, this ADDS to human life and the enjoyment of our years. Our mission statement says that "Saved by grace, we are called to celebrate, SERVE, and make disciples."

God has called each one of us into the MINISTRY. We have ordained ministers but they are not the only ones who do ministry. If that's the case (and it is in many churches), then the church is greatly limited.

No—all people are called by God to use their gifts in service to God and others.

My hope in studying God's vision of the C.H.U.R.C.H. is that each of us can appreciate—no CHERISH—our individual gifts and the gifts of others. And that each of us can use our lives in ministry.

Paul writes, **"The gifts he (God) gave were that some would be apostles, some prophets, some evangelists, some pastors and teachers, to equip the saints for the work of ministry, for building up the body of Christ, until all of us come to the unity of the faith and of the knowledge of the Son of God, to maturity, to the measure of the full stature of Christ."** (Ephesians 4:11-13)

The ordained pastor's main job is **"to equip the saints for the work of ministry."** The ordained pastor is not to DO all the ministry.

This is a concept that is changing very slowly but, if we are to do well for the future, the church has got to understand it and pastors have got to get out of the way so that the people of God can do what their gifts demand.

Some people, for example, have the real gift of hospitality. They are the ones who should be making hospital and shut in calls. Others have the gift of teaching. They need to be leading the classes. Some have gifts of spiritual insight and wisdom. They need to be the leaders in the church. Every spiritual gift needs to be uncovered and used. We've hardly begun and there is much to do. But we're heading in the right direction.

H = HOPE

Where do we find true hope? Where else will people hear the GOOD NEWS that has defeated death? Will the education system do it? Will the government? The military? The family? What about philosophy, psychology, zoology, or anthropology? Will the media be the means of eternal good news and lasting hope? What about the arts? No—the calling of the church is to give this world and its people HOPE.

The early church took off because it proclaimed a message of hope that was not resident in the religion of Rome, Greece, or the local religions of the Middle East. There is something about this man named Jesus and the things he taught and the way he lived his life, died, and rose again that speaks deeply of hope.

And the church is the means of hope.

+ + +

There is a perfect alignment of human need with what the church is called for to provide! The church gives this world CHRIST, a spiritual HOME, URGENCY in getting the good news out there, RELATIONSHIPS people desperately want and need, CALLING into special ministry, and HOPE that outlasts anything this world can offer.

Too often we, THE CHURCH, get off track. We lose our vision of what God is calling us to be and do. We major in minors and act more like a business than the very body of Christ. We can easily get off track.

In Matthew 14 we read about Peter who said, **"'Lord, if it is you, command me to come to you on the water.' He (Jesus) said, 'Come.' So Peter got out of the boat, started walking on the water, and came toward Jesus. But when he noticed the strong wind, he became frightened, and beginning to sink, he cried out, 'Lord, save me!' Jesus immediately reached out his hand and caught him, saying to him, 'You of little faith, why did you doubt?' When they got into the boat, the wind ceased. And those in the boat worshiped him, saying, 'Truly you are the Son of God.'"**

Jesus urges us, the church, to be the church. That means getting out of the boat. It even means walking on water.

We fail when we become afraid and take our eyes off Jesus.

But Jesus is there—with outstretched arms—willing and wanting to lift us up to help us be what we are uniquely called to be.

No church is an accident. Each church is called by God for specific ministry and service. Each church has a duty to discover the specifics of its being the C.H.U.R.C.H.

As we gather for worship. As we meet in L.I.F.E. Groups. As we assemble in annual meetings or for fellowship or service projects, let us keep the vision before us of God's special calling for us in these times.

We're given one shot at life and one shot to make something special of what we call "our church". There are no second chances at being the church. Either we are the church or we are something else.

Too easily we think of ourselves as a business… or an institution… or as a club… or as a privileged people… But "Saved by grace, we are called to Celebrate, Serve and Make Disciples." May God bless us in our mission. Amen.

CHAPTER ONE

C.H.U.R.C.H. – Christ!

EPHESIANS 1:3-14

Blessed be the God and Father of our Lord Jesus Christ, who has blessed us in Christ with every spiritual blessing in the heavenly places, just as he chose us in Christ before the foundation of the world to be holy and blameless before him in love. He destined us for adoption as his children through Jesus Christ, according to the good pleasure of his will, to the praise of his glorious grace that he freely bestowed on us in the Beloved. In him we have redemption through his blood, the forgiveness of our trespasses, according to the riches of his grace that he lavished on us. With all wisdom and insight he has made known to us the mystery of his will, according to his good pleasure that he set forth in Christ, as a plan for the fullness of time, to gather up all things in him, things in heaven and things on earth. In Christ we have also obtained an inheritance, having been destined according to the purpose of him who accomplishes all things according to his counsel and will, so that we, who were the first to set our hope on Christ, might live for the praise of his glory. In him you also, when you had heard the word of truth, the gospel of your salvation, and had believed in him, were marked with the seal of the promised Holy Spirit; this is the pledge of our inheritance toward redemption as God's own people, to the praise of his glory.

JOHN 1:1-18

In the beginning was the Word, and the Word was with God, and the Word was God. He was in the beginning with God. All things came into being through him, and without him not one thing came into being. What has come into being in him was life, and the life was the light of all people. The light shines in the darkness, and the darkness did not overcome it.

There was a man sent from God, whose name was John. He came as a witness to testify to the light, so that all might believe through him. He himself was not the light, but he came to testify to the light. The true light, which enlightens everyone, was coming into the world.

He was in the world, and the world came into being through him; yet the world did not know him. He came to what was his own, and his own people did not accept him. But to all who received him, who believed in his name, he gave power to become children of God, who were born, not of blood or of the will of the flesh or of the will of man, but of God.

And the Word became flesh and lived among us, and we have seen his glory, the glory as of a father's only son, full of grace and truth. (John testified to him and cried out, "This was he of whom I said, 'He who comes after me ranks ahead of me because he was before me.'") From his fullness we have all received, grace upon grace. The law indeed was given through Moses; grace and truth came through Jesus Christ. No one has ever seen God. It is God the only Son, who is close to the Father's heart, who has made him known.

A *small town had three churches: Presbyterian, Methodist, and Lutheran.*
All three had a serious problem with squirrels in the church. Each church in its own fashion had a meeting to deal with the problem.

The Presbyterians decided that it was predestined that squirrels be in the church and that they would just have to live with them.

The Methodists decided they should deal with the squirrels lovingly in the style of Charles Wesley. They humanely trapped them and released them in a park at the edge of town. Within 3 days, they were all back in the church.

The Lutherans confirmed them. They're the only church in town with no squirrel problem!

I have this in my own family. My sister doesn't usually go to church. Several years ago her family and mine were at our Mother's house at the same time. So we all went to church on Sunday.

After church my sister said, "What's the point with the liturgy? I hold this book, don't know where I am and I'm wondering WHY? So I just quit. It doesn't make sense to me."

Then she told me how her recent carpel tunnel surgery made it painful for her to hold the hymnal and how she couldn't really read the words—because the print was too small. Finally she added:

"What's with the service lasting over an hour? Does it really have to last that long?"

You know what I'm talking about. My sister believes she can be a perfectly good Christian without the church. You know and love people like this as do I. Perhaps you wonder sometimes yourself about church. Sometimes I wonder.

Huntsville has many churches and many church-going people. But on Sunday morning, while we worship in our beautiful sanctuary, chances are overwhelming that your next door neighbor is not worshipping anywhere. For years pollsters tell us that 40% of Americans are in church on Sundays. This "fact" has always amazed pastors who pastor churches who may have 1000 on the rolls and 250 in worship. There's at least a 70% chance that the people you work with are not in worship on Sunday morning. And that's attendance in the Bible belt!

Even though nearly ninety percent of Americans claim to be Christian, at least thirty-five percent (and most sociologists suspect it is a much higher number) of those who make such claims do not worship—even on Christmas!

Clearly there is a disconnect. How can Americans be so religious and yet so apathetic about church? How can so many claim to believe in God but not in God's family? Why are so many churches not doing well in a society that is so self-identified as religious—specifically "Christian"?

These questions point to the reasons why we are embarking on this brief study of what it means to be the C.H.U.R.C.H.

I have to confess and I confess it boldly, I BELIEVE IN THE CHURCH! I am passionate about the church. I believe the church is the very hope of the world. I believe the church brings wholeness and health to people. I believe the church—when it truly lives out its calling—can fulfill our deepest spiritual, social and even psychological needs. Furthermore there is solid evidence that church attendance enhances physical health. According to one study, the regular church-attender lives an average of eight years longer than those who seldom, sporadically or never attend. That is significant.

Put it in this context: What if we found a drug that had the same effect? Don't you imagine sales would be out of this world? The company marketing this product would reap billions!

A more recent study done in 2006, detailed in the Journal of the American Board of Family Medicine, revealed an added 1.8-3.1 years to life expectancy for churchgoers.

"There is something about being knit into the type of community that religious communities embody that has a way of mediating a positive health effect," study leader Daniel Hall, a resident in general surgery at the University of Pittsburgh Medical Center, told LiveScience – the science and technology website of New York-based Imaginova.

Also an Episcopal priest, Hall listed possible reasons for the longer life span, including a decrease in the level of stress when involved with religion and being able to make meaning out of life.

Church is good for people even on a physical level. I believe this is verifiable in each day's obituary column. Those with the most active church life just plainly live longer. Add to that the QUALITY of their life—especially their SPIRITUAL, MENTAL, SOCIAL, EMOTIONAL, and other factors—and the church-goer has huge advantages.

We human beings need several things that the church can offer better than anything else:

1) We need a purpose in living. We need to know that life has meaning and that life is worth living.
2) We need to know that there is hope for the future—a future than even death can't take away from us.
3) We need community and intimacy—especially with God but also with one another.
4) We need to affirm our unique selves. Each of us is created as a special, one-of-a-kind MASTERPIECE. Who else can more truthfully affirm this but the church?

Now, in fairness, let me say this also—the church has failed on many counts:

1) We are guilty of taking the dynamic GOOD NEWS of God in Christ and making it BORING! In a busy, multiple-choice world where people can opt out of being bored, the church can become a lesser option.
2) The church has injured people. The sacred bond of trust has been broken time and time again. Church members have hurt one another and the church itself has wounded people. St. Mark's has lived through this nightmare. We know what betrayal feels like.
3) The church has too often been the bastion of rigidity and narrow-mindedness and even bigotry. The church disavowed slavery and racism way too late. It should have led the way to equality among all people but has too often followed and not led.
4) The church has soft peddled Christ's call to service and sacrifice. Too often we have worshiped comfort and security instead of the One who calls us to BOLD CONFIDENCE IN GOD ALONE.

I could go on and on because the church has failed time and time again. You know that's true and so do I. There is a direct link between church apathy, low commitment, and indifference and the failures of the church.

The church has failed to live out God's vision of all we could and should be. That fact remains and that fact fires me up to do all I humanly can do to bring the church in closer alignment with God's glorious vision. There is no doubt in my mind that the church can be all God intends for it to be. I have no doubt that the church could be significantly different and more attractive if it follows God's intentions for it.

Despite its faults, failures and short-comings, the church remains as God's chosen vehicle. Those of us in the church need to do everything we can to live out the vision God gives us to truly BE THE CHURCH.

Many times I have shared with the congregation a basis for helping us claim God's vision for the church. This vision spells out the word C.H.U.R.C.H.

The "C" stands for CHRIST.

The "H" stands for HOME.

The "U" stands for URGENCY.

The "R" stands for RELATIONSHIPS.

The second "C" stands for CALLING.

The second "H" stands for HOPE.

Try to memorize what C.H.U.R.C.H. stands for because that gives each of us a vision, a conceptual framework—a basis—for the kinds of things we must do to make the church a more deeply appealing and satisfying instrument of God's mercy, grace, and truth.

I will take each of these letters and each of these CORE VALUES in the following chapters that will, hopefully, help us get a grip on God's vision for us as a C.H.U.R.C.H.

+ + +

The first CORE VALUE is Christ. He is our foundation; our HOME, our URGENCY, the basis for our RELATIONSHIPS. Serving Him is our CALLING. He is our HOPE. Everything the church is about is founded on Christ. Paul says, in Ephesians 2(19-22):

So then you are no longer strangers and aliens, *(Christ our HOME)* **but you are citizens with the saints and also members of the household of God,** *(Christ, the basis of our RELATIONSHIPS)* built upon the foundation of the apostles and prophets, *(Christ our CALLING)* with Christ Jesus himself as the cornerstone. In him the whole structure is joined together and grows into a holy temple in the Lord; in whom you also are built together spiritually into a dwelling place for God.

The Gospels also refer to Jesus as the Cornerstone (rejected by the world but valued by the church). **"The stone that the builders rejected has become the very head of the corner,"** (1 Peter 2:7b)

Christ is the WORD of God who was there before there was even an earth. As John's Gospel says, **"In the beginning was the Word, and the Word was with God, and the Word was God."** (John 1:1)

When we were baptized and for some people even before we are baptized, Christ entered our life. Listen to Paul as he tells the Ephesians:

"Blessed be the God and Father of our Lord Jesus Christ, who has blessed us in Christ with every spiritual blessing in the heavenly places, just as he chose us in Christ before the foundation of the world..." (Ephesians 3:3-4a)

The sacrament of Holy Baptism is a holy, awesome, mysterious and wonderful miracle of Christ entering the life of an individual.

We call baptism "Christening" because that is when we become IN CHRIST (that's what "Christening" means).

Let's look at how the other letters of C.H.U.R.C.H. all relate back to our Lord Jesus Christ:

HOME

Christ is our spiritual HOME (to use the second letter of the word C.H.U.R.C.H.) because HOME is where we belong. Jesus Christ is uniquely qualified to fill that empty space we often sense when we ask, "IS THAT ALL THERE IS?"

St. Augustine said many years ago, in his Confessions, "You have made us for yourself, O Lord, and our heart is restless until it rests in you." Each of us is created with a God space. I believe it can be argued that all human beings are innately religious (okay, "spiritual").

When Jesus the Christ comes into our lives, he fills that space and answers the emptiness question. Christ brings us HOME.

The church itself is a place where people can know others and be known deeply by others. As more small groups organize around Jesus so that the rampant loneliness and alienation that so many of us experience can be fed by the love of God and the love of other people.

Christ brings us HOME!

URGENCY

Jesus' "Great Commission" brings urgency to what we are about. **"Go therefore and make disciples of all nations, baptizing them in the name of the Father and of the Son and of the Holy Spirit, and teaching them to obey everything that I have commanded you."** (Matthew 28:19-20a)

Even as we look out on a world languishing in meaninglessness and hopelessness, a sense of URGENCY rises within us and, deep within, we want to tell the whole world about Jesus.

We are like beggars who have found food. We want to share it with other hungry people. We just can't keep it to ourselves. That is why the third letter of C.H.U.R.C.H. reminds us of the core value of URGENCY.

Lutherans are great at admitting we are "beggars" (we do "humble" well), but our shyness keeps us from sharing our faith. Our personal piety convincingly tells us that another person's piety is none of our business. This belief is greatly reinforced by modern culture's compelling mantra that "it doesn't matter what you believe. . ." or "your beliefs are as good as my beliefs. Who am I to convince you otherwise?"

Lutherans have never had to "go, make disciples" in order to get church members. Lutherans in America learned a long time ago that future church members were getting off the boats from Germany and Scandinavia. Unfortunately, those boats stopped coming about a hundred years ago. Besides that, the whole business about being the C.H.U.R.C.H. is not really about building churches and getting bigger. It is about living out God's vision and a vital part of that vision of God in Christ is urgency.

RELATIONSHIP

Being Christian is not the same as being a church member. Being a Christian is all about a relationship with Christ. Part of the loneliness that we experience today can be filled by a RELATIONSHIP with Jesus. The fourth letter of the word C.H.U.R.C.H. is the word RELATIONSHIP.

I love the way the hymn puts it:
What a friend we have in Jesus, All our sins and griefs to bear!
What a privilege to carry Ev'rything to God in prayer!
Oh, what peace we often forfeit; Oh, what needless pain we bear—
All because we do not carry Ev'rything to God in prayer!

(Joseph Scriven, 1820-1886, public domain)

He is there for us. He is there in our deepest, darkest night. He is there in the sunshine of our brightest days. He is the One who is our nearest, dearest Friend and companion in our journey through this life.

What I love about Jesus is that he also teaches us deep truths about our RELATIONSHIPS with others.

A man is rescued after 20 years on a desert island. His rescuer is astonished to find that the castaway has built several imposing structures.

"Wow!" the rescuer says. "What's that beautiful stone building overlooking the bay?"

"That's my home," the castaway says.

"And what about that building over there, with the spires?"

"That," the castaway says, "is my church."

"But wait!" the rescuer says, "That building over there, with the bell tower. What is that?"

"That's the church I used to belong to."

Jesus teaches us that we don't run away from relationships but we work through them. The modern church has gotten into a consumer mentality and when things don't go our way we just run away. The result is behavior that is certainly not Christ-like and tends to reinforce modern superficiality.

Jesus, the Christ, teaches us the supreme importance of forgiveness. If we could practice what Jesus preaches about forgiveness, so many ills that beset us would dissipate.

We need to turn to Jesus to have our RELATIONSHIPS restored, built and solidified. As we meet in small groups and study the questions at the end of each chapter, we can all grow deeper in relationship with Jesus AND in relationship with other people.

This book is not meant for individual study. It is meant as a resource for relationships with God as well as others. The Bible makes it clear that loving God means loving our neighbor—and even (perhaps especially)—our enemy.

It is not natural to love enemies. It is not natural to forgive—especially serious injury, insult, embarrassment. It is not natural to stay with relationships through thick and thin. The deepest, most satisfying relationships, happen through Jesus Christ.

CALLING

Jesus also CALLS us—the fifth letter in the word C.H.U.R.C.H.

God has given every one of us unique gifts.

"Every person has a calling; when he tends to it, he pleases God... Live in your calling and be content in your gifts... Whatever your calling demands is holy and a worship pleasing to God." *(Luther, LECTURES ON GENESIS)*

By blood and origin I am all Albanian.
My citizenship is Indian. I am a Catholic nun.
As to my calling, I belong to the whole world.
As to my heart, I belong entirely to the heart of Jesus.
(Mother Teresa)

I would guess that at least eighty percent and more of us do not know our calling. When we find our calling, what joy we shall have! What excitement enters our hearts! When we find God's purpose for our lives, nothing can beat that!

My hope is that we can dig much deeper in the time you spend with this book and in a small group so that every one of us discovers WHY God has placed us on this planet. Uncovering your *purpose* is one of the greatest discoveries a human can ever make. And that discovery is close at hand.

Jesus said, **"I came that they may have life and have it abundantly."** (John 10:10b) That abundant life finds its joy as we do as we are called to do—not what our parents expected us to do or what friends or society expects. Joy comes in doing what feels right, natural, and fun.

HOPE

Finally, Jesus is our HOPE.

Nothing else will last. I have seen with my own eyes the ruins of ancient civilizations. They built enormous monuments so that they could be remembered. They built them of stone in the hope that it would last. But nothing lasts—life doesn't last and the monuments we build will not last. Our families do not last, our jobs do not last, our civilization will not last—nothing lasts—except the One who created us and who is eager to give us HOPE that will not disappoint us in time and in eternity.

As Jesus said, **"Do not let your hearts be troubled. Believe in God, believe also in me." (John 14:1)**

LOOKING AT THE TEXTS

1) What does it feel like to be chosen? (Contrast that to what it feels like to be the one not chosen). [Ephesians 1:3-4]

2) A little girl, when she heard she was adopted, explained to a friend. "My mommy grew me in her tummy but my real mommy grew me in her heart." She understands adoption as a special calling. Discuss what it means to have received the calling ("adoption") of faith in Christ Jesus. [Ephesians 5]

3) Have you ever wondered why "redemption," "forgiveness," and "grace" are such big words in our faith? Discuss. [Ephesians 1:7]

4) How do you feel in relation to Christ right now? Close? Challenged? Distant? Chosen? Rejected? Something else?

5) What about the modern belief that "all roads lead to God" and that we should not try to share our faith with others?

6) Have you ever thought of the "Word of God" as Christ [John 1] or does the "Word" too often mean "words"—namely the Bible?

7) The fact that the Word became flesh and lived among us implies what?

8) How can our small groups, boards, committees, worship services, circles and all our gathering of "two or three" (or "two or three hundred") be more about Christ and less about us?

9) Pray for a Christ-centeredness in your life and in the life of your family. Pray for that same Christ-centeredness in the C.H.U.R.C.H.

CHAPTER TWO

C.H.U.R.C.H. – Home!

ACTS 4:32-37

Now the whole group of those who believed were of one heart and soul, and no one claimed private ownership of any possessions, but everything they owned was held in common. With great power the apostles gave their testimony to the resurrection of the Lord Jesus, and great grace was upon them all. There was not a needy person among them, for as many as owned lands or houses sold them and brought the proceeds of what was sold. They laid it at the apostles' feet, and it was distributed to each as any had need. There was a Levite, a native of Cyprus, Joseph, to whom the apostles gave the name Barnabas (which means "son of encouragement"). He sold a field that belonged to him, then brought the money, and laid it at the apostles' feet.

LUKE 6:46-49

"Why do you call me 'Lord, Lord,' and do not do what I tell you? I will show you what someone is like who comes to me, hears my words, and acts on them. That one is like a man building a house, who dug deeply and laid the foundation on rock; when a flood arose, the river burst against that house but could not shake it, because it had been well built. But the one who hears and does not act is like a man who built a house on the ground without a foundation. When the river burst against it, immediately it fell, and great was the ruin of that house."

Last week we talked about how the 'C' of the word CHURCH stands for Christ and how he is the CORE VALUE of all that we are as C.H.U.R.C.H.

Today we're going to talk about the letter 'H' of the word C.H.U.R.C.H. The letter 'H' stands for HOME.

Home is where the joy is and also where the suffering may be.

A minister did a sermon on marriage. At the end of the service he was giving out small wooden crosses to each married couple. He said, "Place this cross in the room in which you fight the most and you will be reminded of God's commands and you won't argue as much."

One woman came up after the service and said, "You'd better give me five."

You know it was bad by what the advertisement said: "Wedding dress for sale. Worn once by mistake."

I recently heard a story about the mom and dad with a son who was a freshman in college. He blew off his freshman year. He wasn't very responsible, didn't make good grades, squandered his money, and finally came back home. His parents told him, "If you go back to school you'll have to pay your own way."

So he had to work that summer and not go on the family vacation. That was part of his punishment. The family went to Greece that year and mom sent him a postcard, "Dear Son," she wrote. "Today we stood on the mountains where ancient Spartan women sacrificed their defective children. Wish you were here."

A little girl was being punished by eating alone in the corner of the dining room. The family paid no attention to her until they heard her pray: "I thank Thee, Lord, for preparing a table before me in the presence of mine enemies."

HOME is the place where our greatest battles are fought. And if your home is like mine, especially when my kids were little, Sunday morning is scene of the worst battles!

Everyone wants a good home life. I cannot imagine anyone who just doesn't really care what kind of home life they have. Most people want the best but get much less than the best in their home lives.

Children need a good home life for success in life. Study after study shows that the happiest, most self-assured adults usually came from homes that were happy and secure places. Children may seem pretty tough, but they are quite fragile and are utterly dependent on mom and dad for their deepest physical, emotional, social, mental, and spiritual development.

Aristotle said many years ago, "Man is a political animal." We need others. Our first contact with others begins in the home.

So how does life in the "polis" (Greek for "among people", hence "political") happen in ways that build human character? Allow me to share some practical, sensible, biblical advice:

First: Listen to one another.

I could have said, "LOVE one another." But who's going to disagree with that? Here's how love works: "LISTEN to one another."

The best way of showing love is by listening deeply, and sincerely. Sometimes it is called "active listening" because to really listen takes a lot of work. There is no such thing as "passive listening."

How many of us own a VCR? Now—truthfully—how many of us really know how to program one? Why is there a problem with programming the VCR? Is it not because we have not invested the time necessary to really LISTEN to the manufacture's owner's manual?

A man was walking along the beach and found a bottle. He looked around and didn't see anyone so he opened it. A genie appeared and thanked the man for letting him out. The genie said, "For your kindness I will grant you a wish, but only one - none of that three wishes jazz, Okay?"

The man thought for a minute and said, "Well, I have always wanted to go to Hawaii but have never been able to because I'm afraid of flying, and ships make me claustrophobic and ill. I love to drive. So, I wish for a road to be built from here to Hawaii."

This surprised the genie a bit, but after some thought said, "No, I don't think I can do that. Think about the pilings needed to hold up the highway and how deep they would have to be driven to reach the bottom of the ocean. Think of all the pavement and steel and concrete that would be needed. I'm sorry. You will have to choose another wish."

The man thought for a minute and then told the genie, "There is one other thing that I have always wanted. I would like to be able to understand women. What makes them laugh and cry, why do they get upset at us so easily, what are their true desires and needs? Basically... what makes them tick?!?"

The genie stared at him and blinked a couple times. "So, do you want two lanes or four?"

Men—we understand women by LISTENING; women—you understand us by LISTENING. Parents—we understand our children by LISTENING. Listening is LOVE.

James writes: **"You must understand this, my beloved: let everyone be quick to listen, slow to speak, slow to anger."** (James 1:19)

Easily said but for something that sounds so easy to do listening is hard work! Active listening takes deliberate effort, intentional training, and the strong desire to listen lovingly.

Secondly: Keep commitments.

It has been said that we should be "generous with praise, but cautious with promises." Parents need to keep their promises to their children. Spouses need to keep their promises to one another. All of us need to make sure that if we promise, we deliver.

WHY? Because we construct our hopes around promises. When a couple promise to be faithful to each other "until death does us part", security builds in the relationship. When relationships feel secure, our personal anxiety diminishes considerably.

The Bible has some pretty strong statements on the practice of keeping commitments: **"When you make a vow to God, do not delay fulfilling it; for he has no pleasure in fools. Fulfill what you vow. It is better that you should not vow than that you should vow and not fulfill it."** (Ecclesiastes 5:4-5)

Even Jesus says, **"Let your word be 'Yes, Yes' or 'No, No'; anything more than this comes from the evil one."** (Matthew 5:37) James says it a little more forcefully: **"Above all, my beloved, do not swear, either by heaven or by earth or by any other oath, but let your 'Yes' be yes and your 'No' be no, so that you may not fall under condemnation."** (James 5:12)

Making promises means little. Keeping our commitments builds TRUST. If any family or any church is to function well—it must have TRUST. The only way that we can grow is by keeping the commitments we make.

Is it easy? When my son was little I had promised him that the two of us would go to the zoo. I knew that would mean the world to him. But on the day we were to go to the zoo, I still didn't have my Sunday's sermon done. I NEEDED to get that sermon done. It was Saturday, for goodness sake. But I had made a promise to my son.

In my mind I'm thinking, "We could go to the zoo next week..." But my promise to my son was that we would go TODAY.

That sermon is long forgotten, but I'm guessing that day my son and I had together at the zoo is something he still remembers! I sure do.

Keep your commitments. Proverbs 3 says we should wear them like a necklace; and write them down within your heart.

The third piece of advice is this: Give and receive respect.

The late Sen. Jennings Randolph had a little motto on his desk. It said, "The most important lesson you can learn in life is that other people are as real behind their eyes as you are behind yours."

That's another way of saying, RESPECT OTHERS.

Many marriage counselors can tell within ten to fifteen minutes whether a couple is headed for divorce or not. How? By judging the amount of or lack of respect each has for the other.

The more we respect those in our homes and church, the more we can respect ourselves.

"Love one another with mutual affection; outdo one another in showing honor." (Romans 12:10) In other words: RESPECT ONE ANOTHER.

You want to be respected. Most of us would rather be respected than be liked. But for respect to multiply, it must be dished out liberally. As Paul says, **"Outdo one another in showing honor"**

Number four: Offer encouragement.

Paul writes the Thessalonians: **"Therefore encourage one another and build up each other."** (I Thessalonians 5:11)

How does that happen? How can we encourage and build each other? There are some very simple things we can do that encourage:

SMILING. We all know what a difference a smile makes. 'Nough said.

OUR WORDS. "Man doesn't live by bread alone. He also needs buttering up." Our words of encouragement make a huge difference in daily life.

DWELLING ON WHAT IS POSITIVIE. A reporter once asked the great entrepreneur Andrew Carnegie why he hired forty-three millionaires to work for him. Carnegie pointed out that those individuals were not millionaires when he hired them.

The reporter then asked, "How did you develop these men to become so valuable to you that you paid them so much money?"

Carnegie replied that people are developed the same way gold is mined. When gold is mined, several tons of dirt must be moved to get an ounce of gold; but you don't go into the mine looking for dirt—you go in looking for gold.

The same is true with people. Look for what is good. Here again, listen to the Apostle Paul: **"Finally, beloved, whatever is true, whatever is honorable, whatever is just, whatever is pure, whatever is pleasing, whatever is commendable, if there is any excellence and if there is anything worthy of praise, think about these things."** (Philippians 4:8)

The fifth piece of advice is: Ask for and receive forgiveness. We all know the value of forgiveness. We can all understand why people should forgive us when we "forget" something or "overlook" someone or happen to be in a foul mood and say something hurtful. It seems natural because we know our intentions and thoughts.

When it comes to forgiving others, it is always more difficult. Forgiveness is not natural and it is not easy. Some struggle more with this than others but I believe it is safe to say that ALL human beings find forgiveness hard.

There is a story about a Spanish father and son who became estranged. The son left home and the father set out to find him. He searched for months with no success. Finally, in desperation, the father turned to the newspaper for help. His ad said, "Dear Paco, meet me in front of the newspaper office at noon on Saturday. All is forgiven. I love you. Your father." That Saturday, the story goes, hundreds of young men named Paco showed up looking for forgiveness and love from their estranged fathers.

The only way families can flourish and thrive is through forgiveness. The only way the family of God, the C.H.U.R.C.H. can flourish and thrive is through forgiveness. Maybe that is why Jesus made forgiveness the cornerstone of his life and teaching.

+ + +

This study on C.H.U.R.C.H. is about the church—but the church is not a building—it is people like you and me. The church is not primarily an organization—it is a movement. The church is best at home:

The best youth program in the church is the one at home. Young people learn about prayer and worship. They learn to ask questions and find answers. They learn to love as they are loved; to forgive as they are forgiven. In other words—all Christian truths are most effectively taught at home.

The best support group any of us can have is at home. Home is where husbands, wives, children can
1) LISTEN TO ONE ANOTHER,
2) LEARN TO MAKE AND KEEP COMMITMENTS,
3) GIVE AND RECEIVE RESPECT,
4) OFFER ENCOURAGEMENT, and
5) ASK FOR AND RECEIVE FORGIVENESS.

The Christian faith grows best and strongest at home. The CHURCH exists to strengthen all the ministry that is happening in the homes of all our people.

Last week we read about CHRIST. Today we talk about HOME. Next week we'll talk about the "U" of the word "C.H.U.R.C.H.": URGENCY. Now is it time to talk about taking the church out of the building and our homes and into the streets.

The church itself is our HOME

LOOKING AT THE TEXTS

1) In the early church personal needs were placed aside and the needs of the group were given priority. What sounds attractive about this? What is repulsive? [Acts 4:32]
2) How do you suppose the apostles showed "great power"? [Acts 4:33]
3) How would you interpret the passage "great grace was upon them all."? [Acts 4:33]
4) How were such levels of trust achieved that people would hand over all their possessions to the apostles? [Acts 4:34-35]
5) Knowing that names are not accidental in biblical times, what significance do you see in changing "Joseph" into "Barnabus"? [Acts 4:36] How can we raise up Barabuses?
6) The solid foundation of a home or a church is Jesus Christ. [Luke 6:48-49] Why do you suppose Christ makes such a difference?
7) What if Christ is not present? Does it really make a difference?
8) What one thing would make a huge difference in your life if you could do it habitually?
__ Be a great listener
__ Keep every commitment
__ Give and receive respect
__ Offer encouragement
__ Ask for and receive forgiveness
__ Other: _____

CHAPTER THREE

C.H.U.R.C.H. - Urgency

REVELATION 22:20-21

The one who testifies to these things says, "Surely I am coming soon." Amen. Come, Lord Jesus! The grace of the Lord Jesus be with all the saints. Amen.

MATTHEW 28:18-20

And Jesus came and said to them, "All authority in heaven and on earth has been given to me. Go therefore and make disciples of all nations, baptizing them in the name of the Father and of the Son and of the Holy Spirit, and teaching them to obey everything that I have commanded you. And remember, I am with you always, to the end of the age."

I find it interesting that the Bible ends with a strong note of urgency. Actually most of the New Testament is colored with expectation and urgency. The last book of the Bible, Revelation, is an urgent message proclaimed to a world expecting Christ's imminent return.

Now—nearly 2000 years later, we are still waiting. As a result, the urgency that accompanied the early church has disappeared among many Christian groups. Some of the groups that focus on the end, seem to be fringe groups that have histories of predicting dates, setting up expectations, and then either resetting dates (and assuring their own oblivion) or keeping Christ's return as "soon" but with no specifics. The Jehovah's Witnesses and Seventh Day Adventists are prominent groups propagating the end-times expectations. Many fundamentalist, charismatic and Evangelical denominations often beat the end-times drum.

Fear of the end or one's status before God in death is often used to stir up membership. At the Lutheran church I served in Kansas, one of my predecessors had the greatest success in building church attendance. His era was one of envy for all subsequent pastors—at least initially. He, more than any other pastor, filled the pews. When he preached, back in the 1920s, his messages stirred the fear of God in the people attending. When I was pastor of this congregation, some of the members were college students during this pastor's tenure. They told me how terrified they were of Jesus' soon-to-be-expected return.

His successors could not, in good conscience, highlight the fear-tinged theology that filled the pews. I am sure this pastor was sincere—he was just incorrect. His emphasis may have filled the pews, but it did not bring good news to God's people.

I believe escapism is another motive prompting people to highlight the apocalyptic portions of scripture. Sometimes I get the sense that those who most fervently wish for the Lord's imminent return are looking for escape over against hope. As the times rapidly change and things get out of hand, it is comforting to believe that all this will soon pass and God will receive us on a cloud at Jesus' return. There is escape from it all after all.

Yet the Lord calls us to have HOPE and the Lord also calls us to battle—not escape. So long as we are alive, we have a mission. And that mission is URGENT because HOPE itself is in urgent need for a world in a swirl.

The escapist genre of Christian literature has enjoyed enormous success in the United States in the last decade or so. The Left Behind series of novels by Tim LaHaye and Jerry B. Jenkins has sold tens of millions of copies. When USA TODAY did a review of the 13th book of the series in 2005, they described it as "One of the greatest success stories in book publishing." *(USA TODAY, 2/28/2005)*. The late Jerry Falwell said of the initial LEFT BEHIND book: "In terms of its impact on Christianity, it's probably greater than that of any other book in modern times, outside the Bible." *(TIME magazine, 9/8/2007)*. The books were based on a specific eschatological reading of the Christian Bible, particularly the Books of Daniel and Revelation.

The series, while providing great escapist reading, presented the world with some very bad theology. Today many faithful members of Christian churches really believe the Bible says that the world will end soon in a way similar to that depicted in the novels. Christians often seem willing to throw out their belief in a loving, grace-filled God for one who will "rapture" believing airline pilots meanwhile letting the plane crash to the earth killing off all passengers. Christians, who believe in their hearts that God is a God of mercy, willingly suspend that belief for a God who plays cosmic chess with the forces of darkness and delivers vengeance on those who do not play along on the right side.

Well—the world has NOT ended and perhaps will not end for thousands or even millions of years. We know, however, that it *will* indeed end. More specifically, your world and my world will end much sooner than most any of us can imagine.

It is our denial of this fact that keeps the sense of URGENCY away from our personal theology or understanding of Christian eschatology. The atheist "Father of Psychoanalysis" Sigmund Freud postulated that every one of us lives in denial that we shall die. We really can't face it, he says. So to compensate, we try to leave a legacy. Freud himself wanted to leave his legacy as the Father of Psychoanalysis. Interestingly, the two times in his life when he fainted (a bodily reaction to the most powerful denial … the mind completely shuts down in the face of threat) were both when his legacy was threatened.

But we do die and God has given us a mission in this life to complete before we die. There really is URGENCY to our mission. That urgency is not based on fear or escapism. It is an urgency based on grace. That urgency is there for us as individuals as well as for us as a congregation called to be the C.H.U.R.C.H.

There's an old story that goes something like this: Satan and his minions were debating about how to best tempt the world.

"Let's tell the humans that there is no God. . ." That idea floated around a little but everyone in Satan's court decided, "That won't work—humans are too smart to believe that."

"Then let's tell them that God doesn't care. We can show them how much suffering there is in the world and tell them that God just sits in heaven without a care in the world. . ."

Again, there was some lively discussion but they all eventually agreed that this idea wasn't the best way to convince the world either.

Finally, one of the oldest, most trusted of demons suggested that "we tell them that there is no hurry." "Yes!" replied Satan's court. "That's the very best way to prevent God's kingdom from succeeding. THERE'S NO HURRY!"

There *is* a hurry. There is URGENCY.

So what is this URGENCY all about? It is about telling the good news of Jesus to as many people as possible. It is about living the good news so that others can see our witness. It is about building the very kingdom of God that Jesus spoke so often of. It is about living our lives with a focused sense of intention because of the urgency we have come to know.

The club mentality which sees the church as an organization rails against this sense of urgency. After all, the church is a comfortable club of nice people. Why mess that up with people we don't know?

Our club mentality tries desperately to keep the church from getting too large, "because then I won't know everybody..." Our church-as-organization wants to see us "take care of our own..." (Interestingly some of the churches with the finest care of their own people and little outreach, are also some of the most rapidly declining churches). As an organization we expect certain benefits. We expect to be served and to "get what I pay for..."

But when the church is a movement, everything is turned upside-down. Instead of being served, we are asked to serve. Instead of receiving, we give. Instead of fixing something in time and place, we deal with time and place. The organization becomes much less important than the people the organization is called to serve.

Jesus dealt with the organization in his day and aptly illustrated the purpose of the organization by putting forth the Sabbath day as an illustration. His healing on the Sabbath was apparently a difficulty for the religiously-inclined: **"Then he (Jesus) said to them, 'The sabbath**

was made for humankind, and not humankind for the sabbath; so the Son of Man is lord even of the sabbath." (Mark 2:27-28)

Human need is more important than organizational need.

Let me illustrate exactly how URGENCY plays out in the church (as versus the C.H.U.R.C.H.) with this little story from an unknown source:

"It was a beautiful Sunday morning. People were filling the church. As they entered, each received a bulletin filled with announcements, topic of today's sermon, the hymns they would sing and who they would pray for.

An older man entered that church. His clothes were filthy and you could tell that he hadn't had a bath in awhile. His face was covered in whiskers where he had not shaved for a very long time.

When he reached the usher, he removed his tattered old brown hat in respect. His hair was long, dirty and tangled mess. He had no shoes on his feet, and wore only soiled, black socks.

The usher put his fingers to his nose and glared at the old man and said, 'Uh. I'm sorry sir, but I'm afraid we can't let you in. You will distract the congregation and we don't allow anyone to disrupt our service. I'm afraid you'll have to leave.'

The old man looked down at himself and with a puzzled look on his face, he placed his old brown hat back on his head and turned to leave. He was sad as he loved to hear the choir sing praises to the Lord. He loved to watch the little children get up in the front of the church to sing their little songs. He carried in his pocket a small worn out Bible and loved to see if the minister preached a passage from the Bible that the old man had underlined. He was respectful enough and didn't want to cause any commotion, so he hung down his head and walked back down the steps of the big brick church. He sat down on the brick wall near the edge of the church yard and strained to listen through the closed doors and windows to the singing going on in the church. Oh how he wished he could be inside with all the others. A few minutes had passed by when all of a sudden a younger man came up behind him and sat down near him. He asked the old man what he was doing.

He answered, 'I was going to go to church today, but they thought I was filthy and my clothes are old and worn and they were afraid I would disrupt their service. Sorry I didn't introduce myself. My name is George.

The two gentlemen shook hands and George couldn't help but notice that this man had long hair like his. He wore a piece of cloth draped over his body tied with a royal purple sash. He had sandals on his feet, now covered with dust and dirt.

The stranger reached to touch George's shoulder and said, 'Hello, George, don't feel bad because they would not let you in. My name is Jesus and I've been trying to get into this same church for years, and they won't let me in either." [Source Unknown.]

In this book we are talking about the C.H.U.R.C.H. At the center of the church is Jesus, the Christ. Jesus, as we read the New Testament, had a tendency to hang around with the "wrong kind of people." He paid respect to the disreputable people of the land: prostitutes, outcasts, the lame, the deaf—the utterly despised tax collectors. Jesus even dared touch the dead.

As we seek to live out God's vision of the C.H.U.R.C.H.—Christ is the very center of all that we are and do. In his name we reach out to and welcome all people because we know that every person is precious in God's eyes. Perhaps those rejected by others are even more precious to God?

We began this study with Christ. Last chapter we talked about how the C.H.U.R.C.H. is our HOME and has to get out of the "God box" and that it does its best work in our homes.

The church has to get out of the God box and into our homes but it also has to get out of our homes and into the streets.

We have said that YOU ARE THE CHURCH. The building is merely the "God box" where the church gathers on Sundays and at other times. The organizational structure too often secures us as an *organization* but protects us from being what God has called us to be—namely—a *movement*.

Even though most of the Christian churches in the United States are declining in membership and vitality, most church members say they want the church to grow—to gain in worship attendance (one of the two visible measurements [the other being giving]).

There are several motivations for church growth:

If the church grows, then it confirms our worth as a group of people.

If the church grows, then it means we belong to something dynamic and exciting.

If the church grows, then we have more of an assurance of a future. It has been estimated that three-thousand churches will close per year in this decade. Within the next ten years tens of thousands of churches will close their doors forever. But if we are growing, then our future is more assured and we know that all we put into this thing called the church will last.

Pastors tend to see church growth as visible confirmation of their effectiveness in ministry. "If the church is growing then that indicates I must be an effective leader… preacher…teacher…"

I find it interesting that nearly everyone (especially pastors) *wants* the church to grow, but very few people in the church (again, especially pastors) really want to do the kind of things and put up with the consequences of a church that is growing.

So often, when a church actually does grow, there is a huge displacement of people who long for the days when "I knew everybody…" or "Everything made sense then…" It is not at all unusual for growing churches to have conflict—sometimes severe conflict. People who had a secure place in the organization, have less security (or seniority) in the movement.

A growing church is very similar to a rubber band that is stretched. The rubber band wants to relieve its tension and return to its pre-stretch mode. So do growing churches. This longing for the way it was is an immense obstacle in church growth. But rubber bands were created to stretch. When a rubber band can no longer stretch, it has outlived its usefulness and is tossed away. Likewise a church that refuses to be stretched.

Ironically, the church is NOT about numbers or even growth. The church is certainly not A BUILDING. YOU are the church. I am the church. And the way the church grows is by growing spiritually.

Some time back the cover of TIME magazine was entitled, "The Science of Happiness." The cover story article related religion and happiness: "Studies show that the more a believer incorporates religion into daily living—attending services, reading Scripture, praying— the better off he or she appears to be on two measures of happiness: frequency of positive emotions and overall sense of satisfaction with life. Attending services has a particularly strong correlation to feeling happy, and religious certainty—the sense of unshakable faith in God and the truth of one's beliefs—is most closely linked with life satisfaction." *(TIME, 1/17/2005)*

Later on that same article talks about the church activity in this way: "A 2003 national study involving 3,300 adolescents found that teens who attend services, read the Bible and pray feel less sad or depressed, less alone, less misunderstood and guilty and more cared for than their nonreligious peers."

Sunday worship, Bible study, prayer--for happiness and for spiritual growth. Notice the quality of URGENCY in these dynamics. URGENCY indicates that *something is happening NOW!*

If the church—that's YOU and me—is growing spiritually, then the congregation—will grow numerically. I cannot conceive that God would ever will a congregation to stagnate and decline. As a *spiritual* movement, the church is always about growth—especially *spiritual* growth. And the spiritual and numerical growth of the church grows the very kingdom of God Jesus referred to so often.

How do we grow spiritually? A spiritually growing person *relishes* the GOOD NEWS of Jesus Christ. That good news becomes the highest priority. It also reflects that person's greatest joy. Indeed that good news moves to the very center of his or her life. As Jesus said, that good news is a light that cannot and will not be hidden.

Here is a shocker for many of us shy Lutherans: spiritual growth generally means we cannot remain silent about Jesus. God can't be kept in the God box. Instead God goes home and finds residence there. God is in the neighborhood. God is at family reunions and patio parties.

URGENCY develops in the spiritually-growing person to TELL THE WORLD!

It is that sense of URGENCY to share the GOOD NEWS that brings us to the third letter of the word C.H.U.R.C.H. There is an URGENCY about being the church when the church truly follows God's vision. We simply have to get the WORD out. Beggars telling other beggars where to find (true spiritual) food.

I say this not to make you feel guilty for not being an evangelist. As a naturally shy person myself, it isn't easy for me to tell the good news and I'M ORDAINED! But as I grow spiritually, it becomes easier and more natural for me to share that good news within me with people I genuinely care about.

The key to developing the sense of URGENCY is growing spiritually. Usually spiritual growth happens when we step outside our comfort zone. I have seen people grow spiritually by tithing. I have seen inactive, occasional pew-sitters, become fervent followers of Jesus by getting up and going to church *every* Sunday morning. Getting out of our comfort zones would be like fishermen leaving their nets for larger prey. Jesus called the Apostles and said to them, **"Follow me, and I will make you fish for people."** (Matthew 4:19). Comfort zone be damned.

Jesus calls us to do everything we can to reach out to others with the GOOD NEWS.

Too often we place barriers before people and begin thinking that the God Box is ours. "After all, this is OUR church!" The barriers are not usually intentional. Too often the barriers we place to keep people out of church are on the subconscious level. Too often we rationalize and make excuses for keeping some people away from the good news.

My mother belonged to a little church in a small town in Kansas— Holy Shepherd Lutheran Church. It was a small church with a great *family* feeling. I loved going there. I preached there several times. I even baptized my nephew there.

But they had a problem—someone had invited some residents of a home for the mentally challenged which was down the street—to church. At first it was one man. Then several more started coming. That home had adopted that little church as its spiritual home.

But the good folks of Holy Shepherd didn't want those kinds of people attending their church.

Well—the good folks of Holy Shepherd no longer have to worry about attracting the wrong kind of people to their church because their church had to close its doors several years ago. The building is now a community building and all kinds of people are invited.

There is a kind of idolatry when we start speaking about "OUR church". The church never belongs to us—rather we belong to Christ. It is God's church. And if the body of people calling itself the church chooses to not follow God's vision of what it means to be church, then that church's days are probably numbered—no matter how large they are or how beautiful their buildings.

God calls us to do everything we possibly can to reach out to those who are lost to God. Reaching the unchurched is the most important thing a church can do. It deserves top place in the budget and in all programming.

FIRST, it means that everything we do and all the decisions we make as a church must be made with this question in mind: WHAT WILL ATTRACT THOSE WHO ARE FAR FROM GOD? WHAT WILL BRING PEOPLE CLOSER TO GOD? For example, is there anything we can do to make our Sunday morning experience an experience that attracts those who are far from God? Is there someone in worship on a typical Sunday morning that I don't know? I need to reach out with the handshake of friendship and friendliness to those I don't know. The time for associating with our close friends in church is in small fellowship groups and Bible studies—but Sunday morning is a time to REACH OUT to those who may be friendless or who may be searching for meaning and truth that comes through Jesus Christ.

SECONDLY, it means we've got to get OUT OF THE GOD BOX.

Jesus met unbelievers where they were. He realized what many Christians today never seem to. According to one count, the gospel records 132 contacts that Jesus had with people. Six were in the Temple, four in the synagogue and 122 were out with people in the mainstream of life. [J.K. Johnston. Why Christians Sin. (Discovery House, 1992) p. 142]

THIRD, and most importantly, it means GROWING SPIRITUALLY.

A=Attend worship weekly.

B=Bible reading

C=Communicating with God

As we grow spiritually, the URGENCY of the GOOD NEWS will be a natural development.

The GOOD NEWS cannot be kept hidden. What happened when Andrew heard Jesus? The first thing he did was tell his brother Simon, **"We have found the Messiah."** (John 1:41).

Christ our Lord calls us to reach out to a world lost in meaninglessness and purposelessness. Christ our Lord calls us to be the CHURCH. And the "U" in that word stands for URGENCY.

LOOKING AT THE TEXTS

1) What do you suppose John meant when he wrote in the last chapter of the Bible, **"The one who testifies to these things says, 'Surely I am coming soon.' Amen. Come, Lord Jesus!"?** [Revelation 22:20]
2) Does the expectation of Jesus' coming say much to us today? If so, what? Is there any way we can capture at least a part of the sense of URGENCY exhibited in the New Testament?
3) Is it really true that "If the church—that's YOU and me—is growing spiritually, then the congregation—will grow numerically." (p. 42) Discuss.
4) How do churches place barriers before people that hinder church growth? How do WE place barriers that hinder growth?

5) How can we help lower or eliminate those barriers?
6) What are our motivations in seeking to fulfill the Great Commission?

___ Obedience to Jesus' command

___ Love of all people and the desire they also experience the Good News we have experienced in Christ.

___ To grow the church

7) Jesus has promised that disciple making is not a lone-ranger thing to do. In fact he promised, **"I am with you always, to the end of the age."** [Matthew 28:20]
8) How can this group help you be a witness? How can you help the church in its witness?

CHAPTER FOUR

C.H.U.R.C.H. – **Relationships**

DEUTERONOMY 6:4-5

Hear, O Israel: The Lord is our God, the Lord alone. You shall love the Lord your God with all your heart, and with all your soul, and with all your might

MATTHEW 22:27-40

"You shall love the Lord your God with all your heart, and with all your soul, and with all your mind.' This is the greatest and first commandment. And a second is like it: "You shall love your neighbor as yourself.' On these two commandments hang all the law and the prophets."

JOHN 13:34-35

"I give you a new commandment, that you love one another. Just as I have loved you, you also should love one another. By this everyone will know that you are my disciples, if you have love for one another"

Last chapter dwelt on the "Great Commission" and this chapter deals with the "Great Commandment"—the other "Great" initiated by Christ our Lord.

The "*shema*" as it is called, from Deuteronomy 6, is the most sacred text of Judaism. This passage deals with our relationship to God. The New Testament equivalent is the "Great Commandment" of Jesus to not only love God but neighbor as self.

It has been said that if a church only observes the two "Greats" of our Lord, that church will thrive. The impulse to tell the good news (the "Great Commission") combined with the unworldly attraction of self-giving love (the "Great Commandment") is powerful.

Loving others is not always easy. There are several reasons for the difficulty in loving others. Perhaps the most common reason is that we confuse "love" with a feeling rather than a decision.

Love as a feeling is propagated by popular media. But love as a decision is biblical. Jesus said this in a most profound way: **"…I say to you that listen, Love your enemies, do good to those who hate you, bless those who curse you, pray for those who abuse you."** (Luke 6:27-28)

It is one thing to love a friend or family member and have wonderful, warm feelings toward that person or those people, but it is quite another to love someone who seeks your harm and perhaps even your life. Only a willful decision can love such a person. Jesus asks, **"If you love those who love you, what credit is that to you? For even sinners love those who love them.** (Luke 6:32). In effect Jesus is saying, "Do something quite extraordinary—love the unlovable."

The love that Jesus commanded was *agape* love — that was the Greek word in the original Biblical manuscripts — *agape*. *Agape* love isn't some sort of sentimental feeling, which is the way that we usually think of love. No—love is a decision; love is an action. Love is more than a feeling. That's one reason we misunderstand the meaning of love as Jesus spoke about it.

Another reason we give for not loving people is because they don't "deserve" it. Perhaps they are mean-spirited, spiteful, greedy, gossips. Some people are plainly repulsive. The person living under the freeway overpass has not had a bath in months. His hair is matted. Some of his front teeth are missing from a combination of Meth use and fist fights. His brain has clearly been fried by drug and alcohol abuse. Yet—this man is also a child of the Most High. Is he deserving of this exalted position? Of course not. But do you know anyone who is deserving? The bottom line is that NONE of us "deserves" God's love. Yet God still loves. It's called "grace."

Again that *agape* love is in effect. Love that *decides* and love that *acts*.

Too easily we make excuses for not *deciding* and for not *acting*. The people who don't "deserve" to be loved for one reason or another are almost always the very people that need love the most.

I had a situation recently with a person I considered very unfriendly, aloof, and critical of others and me too. Every conversation with this person seemed negative. So, I simply avoided this individual.

Meanwhile, someone had mentioned to me that this same individual was experiencing severe depression and would I pray for her? Suddenly the light came on in my head: "depression"? "Pray for her"? Here was a person in need of love; in need of ministry. And me? I was ignoring that need; turning my back on it and judging the person harshly.

I learned a long time ago that "Hurting people hurt." Hurting people; wounded people, will be nasty, critical, judgmental, and un-loveable. They can really hurt and wound others. Yet they are the very people Christ loves and sent me to love as well. I fail as a Christian when I ignore, shun or—even worse—heap more judgment upon a person already judged and condemned by his or her own deep woundedness.

The next time I saw this woman, I *deliberately, willfully* reached out to her with a smile, handshake, and friendly words. And she responded in a way that made me feel good inside.

Not every hurting person will respond positively. Many times— perhaps more often than not—he or she will respond with more hurt. But Christ's love calls us to love especially the unlovable.

+ + +

Previously I wrote about the ABC's of spiritual growth:
- ATTENDING worship without excuse each Sunday.
- BIBLE reading without excuse every day.
- CONVERSATION with God without excuse every day.

It is incredibly easy to make excuses for ourselves.

Two men, fishing on Sunday morning, were feeling guilty. Said one, "I suppose we should have stayed home and gone to church."

The other replied, "Heck, I couldn't have gone to church anyway. My wife's in bed with the flu." *(From The Funny Side of Fishing, by Jim Reed, The Joyful Noiseletter, June-July '97)*

Today we're going to talk about something that will also elicit tremendous EXCUSES from each of us—I very much include myself in this. We EXCUSE ourselves from any depth of relationship with others.

A touching story came to me by e-mail. As with many "forwards" one gets off the computer, I cannot vouch for the authenticity or truthfulness of the story, but it makes a great point and points to a great truth:

One day, when I was a freshman in high school, I saw a kid from my class was walking home from school. His name was Kyle. It looked like he was carrying all of his books. I thought to myself, "Why would anyone bring home all his books on a Friday? He must really be a nerd." I had quite a weekend planned (parties and a football game with my friends tomorrow afternoon), so I shrugged my shoulders and went on.

As I was walking, I saw a bunch of kids running toward him. They ran at him, knocking all his books out of his arms and tripping him so he landed in the dirt. His glasses went flying, and I saw them land in the grass about ten feet from him. He looked up and I saw this terrible sadness in his eyes.

My heart went out to him. So, I jogged over to him and as he crawled around looking for his glasses, and I saw a tear in his eye. As I handed him his glasses, I said, "Those guys are jerks. They really should get lives."

He looked at me and said, "Hey thanks!" There was a big smile on his face. It was one of those smiles that showed real gratitude. I helped him pick up his books, and asked him where he lived. As it turned out, he lived near me, so I asked him why I had never seen him before. He said he had gone to private school before now. I would have never hung out with a private school kid before. We talked all the way home, and I carried his books. He turned out to be a pretty cool kid. I asked him if he wanted to play football on Saturday with me and my friends. He said yes.

We hung out all weekend and the more I got to know Kyle, the more I liked him. And my friends thought the same of him. Monday morning came, and there was Kyle with the huge stack of books again. I stopped him and said, "Damn boy, you are gonna really build some serious muscles with this pile of books everyday!" He just laughed and handed me half the books.

Over the next four years, Kyle and I became best friends. When we were seniors, we began to think about college. Kyle decided on Georgetown, and I was going to Duke. I knew that we would always be friends, that the miles would never be a problem. He was going to be a doctor, and I was going for business on a football scholarship. Kyle was valedictorian of our class. I teased him all the time about being a nerd. He had to prepare a speech for graduation. I was so glad it wasn't me having to get up there and speak.

Graduation day, I saw Kyle. He looked great. He was one of those guys that really found himself during high school. He filled out and actually looked good in glasses. He had more dates than I did and all the girls loved him!

Boy, sometimes I was jealous. Today was one of those days, I could see that he was nervous about his speech. So, I smacked him on the back and said, "Hey, big guy, you'll be great!" He looked at me with one of those looks (the really grateful one) and smiled. "Thanks," he said.

As he started his speech, he cleared his throat, and began. "Graduation is a time to thank those who helped you make it through those tough years.

"Your parents, your teachers, your siblings, maybe a coach... but mostly your friends. I am here to tell all of you that being a friend to someone is the best gift you can give them. I am going to tell you a story." I just looked at my friend with disbelief as he told the story of the first day we met.

He had planned to kill himself over the weekend. He talked of how he had cleaned out his locker so his mom wouldn't have to do it later and was carrying his stuff home. He looked hard at me and gave me a little smile. "Thankfully, I was saved. My friend saved me from doing the unspeakable."

I heard the gasp go through the crowd as this handsome, popular boy told us all about his weakest moment. I saw his mom and dad looking at me and smiling that same grateful smile. Not until that moment did I realize its depth

Never underestimate the power of your actions. With one small gesture you can change a person's life, for better or for worse. God puts us all in each other's lives to impact one another in some way. Look for God in others.

This man was living out the fourth letter of the word C.H.U.R.C.H.: RELATIONSHIPS. He was exhibiting a deliberate, willful, non-emotional love that we call "friendship."

We all need FRIENDSHIP—relations with other people. It is a basic human need. We need to care about others and have others care about us. We need to know and accept other people and have other people know and accept us.

There are many things that keep us from our deepest human needs: We are too busy to really care deeply and to know and accept other people other than perhaps just a few. Our jobs demand more of us—more of our time and more of our energy. There is less time available for friendships.

In a survey of several hundred senior executives and managers throughout the U.S. conducted by NFI Research, "a U.S.-based research firm that identifies and analyzes trends and attitudes in business, organizational management and information technology," ninety-three percent of senior executive and managers are working nine or more hours per day, and seventy percent are working ten or more hours.

For executives and managers, the forty-hour work week is non-existent, with ninety-seven percent of respondents saying they work forty-one hours or more per week, and sixty-four percent saying they work more than fifty hours per week.

Several decades ago "experts" declared that all the "LABOR SAVING" devices being invented would cut the work week down to thirty or fewer hours. As often happens—the "experts" were wrong. It seems that none of the experts anticipated globalization and world-wide competition for jobs and resources.

Priorities get misplaced and relationships seem so difficult that we fill our time and energy with entertainment--television, games, computers/ internet, sports—active involvement or passive entertainment: all keep us from one another. We don't have to deal with others because we can have some degree of human interaction with no downside (unless you want to count the isolation and loneliness that comes from human interaction via the television, computer, or e-mail—or text-messaging [a favorite with the young especially]).

Even our homes keep us from what other generations enjoyed. Years ago sidewalks connected neighbors to one another. But since we drive everywhere, sidewalks became an unnecessary expense and many communities opted out of putting them in.

Years ago telephones systems were often "Party lines." One person could be speaking to another not even knowing how many other people were eaves-dropping on the conversation. It was invasion of privacy, but the upside was more a sense of connectedness.

Most homes in the past had a functioning front porch where folks could enjoy deep conversation and friendships. The front porch was a way people kept cool before air conditioning. More importantly, it was a great way to keep in touch with others. Relationships were richer, more fulfilling.

I have such fond memories of when I was a boy and every summer evening was spent on the front porch talking. We talked about all kinds of things and my dad especially told stories of his childhood, people he had known, and experiences he had had.

Often we had relatives and friends over to our house to swap stories and swat mosquitoes—on the front porch.

Many of us have either never learned or have forgotten the lost art of conversation. We just don't know how to talk about anything but the weather or sports.

We don't know how to share our deepest fears, fondest hopes, most noble aspirations, and our greatest joys. We don't know how to deal with differences of opinion and conflict. We don't know how to discuss the things that matter most. We don't know how to love and accept one another despite what is said. The result is a profound sense of isolation and loneliness.

The church is the place where RELATIONSHIPS can develop and friendships can flourish. At least that's the way it once was. Could it be that way again? Probably not—at least not the way it once was. Especially on Sunday morning—with worship alone. Even if you throw in a Sunday school or discussion group, chances are the walls of isolation would not come down (although they may be lowered some).

The church operates best in small groups centered in PRAYER and GENUINE CARE FOR ONE ANOTHER.

Most people have conversations about the weather, football, or politics. Most of us know precious little about others and others know precious little about us. The face-to-face, honest-to-goodness sharing that shatters the walls that imprison us comes when we take the risk to love and be loved; to share and to keep confidences.

+ + +

There is a second RELATIONSHIP we all need and that is FRIENDSHIP with God. As we said earlier, every human being has a God-place that can be filled with only true worship of the One, true God.

We can try to fill the God-space with activities, or things, or security, or entertainment—but, as St. Augustine said, "Our hearts are restless until they find their rest in Thee."

We can try to ignore the God-space, but it won't go away.

Some people are afraid of the God-space in their hearts because it may mean they will have to change. Perhaps it means they will have to give up something they don't want to give up. Usually it means giving up control.

Many people have lived so long with an empty God-space that it feels natural—except for that spiritual voice that speaks in the silence before slumber and in the beauty of a sunrise.

One of the most beautiful and meaningful—yet profoundly simple hymns is "Jesus Loves me."

Karl Barth, the great theologian once remarked that his entire theology could be summed up in that one simple hymn.

Another hymn of spiritual friendship is "What a Friend We Have in Jesus" by Joseph M. Scriven:

What a Friend we have in Jesus, all our sins and griefs to bear!
What a privilege to carry everything to God in prayer!
O what peace we often forfeit, O what needless pain we bear,
All because we do not carry everything to God in prayer.
Have we trials and temptations? Is there trouble anywhere?
We should never be discouraged; take it to the Lord in prayer.
Can we find a friend so faithful who will all our sorrows share?
Jesus knows our every weakness; take it to the Lord in prayer.
Are we weak and heavy laden, cumbered with a load of care?
Precious Savior, still our refuge, take it to the Lord in prayer.
Do your friends despise, forsake you? Take it to the Lord in
    prayer!
In His arms He'll take and shield you; you will find a solace there.

(Text in public domain: Joseph Scriven, 1820-1886)

There is no friendship like friendship with God and that friendship comes through God's own Son Jesus. In him the barriers have been broken down. He has bridged the chasm that separates us. True at-onement (atonement) is achieved.

+ + +

How can we develop all our important relationships?

First, understand that RELATIONSHIPS can be hard. People can and will say and do hurtful things. It is difficult to trust people: if you share your innermost self with others, will they still love you and respect you? Or—will they use this information to stab you in the back?

When you have done or said something hurtful, will others forgive you as you imagine yourself forgiving them? FORGIVENESS IS HUGE! Whole books have been devoted to developing the ability to forgive. Some people spend thousands of dollars going to therapists because of their inability to forgive a past hurt. Let it never be said that the church is 'mean spirited' or 'unforgiving'—the church is best positioned to practice the difficult art of FORGIVNESS and creating a safe place for people to be real.

People can betray us and turn on us and use our own words against us—that's fact! But the power—and it is an immense power—to forgive resides in each of us as individuals and in all of us as the church. That immense spiritual power is a most worthy goal for every Christian and every Christian church.

Since relationships are difficult, the only way they can grow deeply is by trust and time together.

That means we have got to make the COMMITMENT to spend time with others. Time is that most precious human resources that will run out for all of us sooner than we think. It is very easy to say, "I don't have time for friendships."

The bottom line is that we all have enough time to do everything that each of us considers important. Relationships are important.

Secondly it means learning to trust others by sharing ever deeper parts of ourselves with others.

Have you noticed that when you are around a person who is very open and sharing, you feel a sense of greater relaxation (unless they get too personal too soon)? Likewise, a person who never says anything tends to put a damper on a sense of openness and sharing. You just don't know where he or she is coming from.

There are naturally shy persons and they especially need to be drawn out and encouraged to feel relaxed in a group. They need to know they are valued. They need trust more than anybody. Trust grows as we learn to share more deeply of ourselves.

And when we do that we learn that we are all so much more alike than different. When we never share, we sense that we alone have this issue or problem. But sharing brings out others' struggles with the same issue or problem.

Make time, build trust.

Therefore I want to propose to you two action items: One, get into a care group. You deserve the best! If you are not currently in a group, join one today.

Put this promise on your refrigerator or bathroom mirror—someplace where you will see it frequently.

Then as care groups get organized, make no more excuses—get involved!

The second thing you can do that can help improve your relationships: especially with God and family is this: A, B, C. . . .

Attend worship weekly. Engage in Bible reading daily. Here's a practical way to do Bible reading and Communicate with God in a way that builds RELATIONSHIPS:

Have family or couple devotions using one of many devotional books or booklets available.
- Do this around the table at supper time.
- Do this at breakfast
- Do this in the evening, before going to bed.
- MAKE IT A HABIT!

Two kinds of RELATIONSHIPS develop—the vertical one (with God) and the horizontal ones (with one another).

We have a friend who is above every friend—his name is Jesus.

LOOKING AT THE TEXTS

1) Why do you suppose the *"Shema"* [Deuteronomy 6:4ff.] is considered the most important prayer in Judaism? *(It is used twice a day as a morning and evening prayer).*

2) How might a twice-daily recitation of the Great Commandment serve a similar function in Christian circles as we seek to be the C.H.U.R.C.H.?

3) How much of our *identity* is tied to the Great Commission and the Great Commandment?

4) Imagine and, as a group, brain storm the effect of living out the two "Greats" (especially in this context, the "Great Commandment") on our witness to the world . . .

5) What keeps us from more fully living out the relational component of our faith? *(Name as many factors you can think of and list them on paper).*
6) What practical *decisions* can you and your group make that would help you love more fully?
7) What steps can our congregation take that would give us a more loving witness to the world?

CHAPTER FIVE

C.H.U.R.C.H. – **Calling**

MARK 2:13-17

Jesus went out again beside the sea; the whole crowd gathered around him, and he taught them. As he was walking along, he saw Levi son of Alphaeus sitting at the tax booth, and he said to him, "Follow me." And he got up and followed him.

And as he sat at dinner in Levi's house, many tax collectors and sinners were also sitting with Jesus and his disciples—for there were many who followed him. When the scribes of the Pharisees saw that he was eating with sinners and tax collectors, they said to his disciples, "Why does he eat with tax collectors and sinners?" When Jesus heard this, he said to them, "Those who are well have no need of a physician, but those who are sick; I have come to call not the righteous but sinners."

EPHESIANS 4:11-13

The gifts he gave were that some would be apostles, some prophets, some evangelists, some pastors and teachers, to equip the saints for the work of ministry, for building up the body of Christ, until all of us come to the unity of the faith and of the knowledge of the Son of God, to maturity, to the measure of the full stature of Christ.'

ISAIAH 6:8

Then I heard the voice of the Lord saying, "Whom shall I send, and who will go for us?" And I said, "Here am I; send me!"

A man had 50 yard line tickets for the big playoff game. As he takes his seat in the bleachers, another man comes down and asks if anyone is sitting in the seat next to him.

"No," he says, "The seat is empty."

"This is incredible," said the man. "Who in their right mind would have a seat like this for the big playoff game, and not use it?"

He says, "Well, actually, the seat belongs to me. I was supposed to come with my wife, but she passed away. This is the first playoff game we haven't been to together since we got married in 1977."

"Oh, I'm sorry to hear that. That's terrible. But couldn't you find someone else -- a friend or relative, or even a neighbor to take the seat?"

The man shakes his head. "No, they're all at the funeral."

Americans love winners. Football clearly marks winners and losers and the big playoff games, the bowl games and the run for the Super Bowl all point to the winning team.

At the last Super Bowl game, advertisers paid $2.4 million for a thirty second ad! That's $4.8 million a minute! Why? Because they know that nearly ninety million tuned in last year and they expect that perhaps that many or more will tune in this year as well.

We love WINNERS. The winners of the Super Bowl will reap millions. The advertisers will sell multi-millions of goods and services. WE LOVE WINNERS. The world has always loved winners.

What is remarkable about Jesus is that he didn't go for the winners. He didn't seek the hot shots, the talented professionals. Jesus, it seems, loved common people. More than that, it seems that Jesus deliberately sought what most people in his time would call losers! He has crowds of people around him. Hundreds of wonderful people around him. Good people, religious people, dedicated people, competent people.

But Jesus calls Levi, Son of Alphaeus—a tax collector for goodness sake! Everyone was shocked! A tax collector is the lowest of the low: dishonest, greedy, anti-patriotic, collaborator with the Romans. "Why tax collectors and sinners?" people wanted to know. "With so many good people you could have chosen, why them?"

The problem is not only with Jesus calling Levi. It's all the unlikely people he called. If you want to turn the world upside down, you don't start with Galilean fisherfolk--people like Simon (whom Jesus renamed "Rocky": Peter), James, Andrew, John, Phillip and the others. You don't normally want a terrorist like Simon the Zealot as part of your team. No—you use sense and appoint rational, decent people like Judas whose very name signifies that he is a fine fellow in good standing.

Jesus is still calling the most unlikely of people. Perhaps Jesus is calling YOU? (Hint: if you are a follower, a Christian, you can know he *is* calling you.) There is no longer any room for an abstract, Sunday morning, cultural "Christianity." And Jesus calls you to no less a calling than turning the world upside down.

Too often when we think of calling, we think of calling into the ministry: PROFESSIONAL MINISTRY. But to really understand God's vision of the C.H.U.R.C.H., we have to understand that "Calling" is for all those who are disciples of the Lord Jesus Christ!

Listen to the Apostle Paul: **"The gifts he gave were that some would be apostles, some prophets, some evangelists, some pastors and teachers, to equip the saints for the work of ministry, for building up the body of Christ, until all of us come to the unity of the faith and of the knowledge of the Son of God, to maturity, to the measure of the full stature of Christ.** (Ephesians 4:11-13)

If I understand that passage rightly (and I think I do), then it means that the job of the "professional" (whether that be apostle, or prophet, or pastor or teacher)—is to **"equip the saints for the work of ministry."**

The pastor's job is not to DO THE MINISTRY, but it is to train and help YOU do the ministry. The pastor's (and other "professional" church workers) job is to help you understand your calling. The pastor's job is to help you hear God calling you to serve him with your time, talents, abilities, skills, and life experiences.

Too often I have been guilty of falling into the expectations of traditional ministry: the pastor preaches the sermons, administers the Sacraments, calls on the sick, prays with the dying, and, meanwhile, lay people serve on committees and boards.

No doubt "professional ministers" have held back the church of God more than anything because they do the ministry. Over the years a mentality has developed that, if someone was sick, the professional minister had to call on that person. If a lesson had to be taught, the professional minister had to teach. If something had to get done, the professional minister had to do it. If prayers are needed, the professional minister needs to say the prayers.

So the bottle-neck of the church is the professional!

When Michael Slaughter was called to Ginghamsburg United Methodist Church in tiny Tipp City, Ohio, it was a little rural congregation. The church had been there for years. They didn't even have indoor toilets. It was a little church in a little town. Everyone knew that a little church in a little town had a little future.

But Michael Slaughter knew that God had called him to Ginghamsburg with a God-size vision. He saw that the church could truly be a C.H.U.R.C.H. It could be God's vision and not the traditional vision of a rural church that was inevitably going to grow older and smaller and eventually, like thousands of other small churches, die out.

Today Ginghamsburg is a huge church of around 5,400 attending (but only 1300 are actually considered members because one must tithe and be sincerely committed to Christian service to be a member).

Size is not a problem for Ginghamsburg's pastor: "Jesus left planet Earth with a church of only 120 people," he said. "So for Jesus, there must be another measurement." People drive miles to attend Ginghamsburg. It is a true magnet church. This individual congregation is accomplishing things in that part of Ohio that is changing lives in a dramatic way. There's something about faith that God is up to something grand that really attracts and moves people.

Several years ago I attended a conference at Ginghamsburg and heard Pastor Slaughter tell the kinds of changes that had to happen for the church to bust out of its old, dying ways.

One thing that had to happen is that the people of God in that place had to claim their calling. For example, Pastor Slaughter said to our group of senior pastors that he was not a very "Pastoral" type of pastor. In other words, as he explained it, "I don't do hospital calls. I don't have the gift of empathy."

As you can imagine, this caused some real problems in the congregation. Everyone knows that the pastor's job is to call on the sick and shut in. Half the people left because Pastor Slaughter's vision of ministry didn't fit their pre-conceptions.

They were down to about 25 people attending on a Sunday morning. But Pastor Slaughter knew that God calls all people into ministry and that there were people within the congregation who had the gift of empathy and could do a wonderful job of calling.

Virtually every growing church has claimed God's vision of C.H.U.R.C.H. and understands that the second "C" stands for CALLING.

People have tried to understand how the Mormons are growing so rapidly. Around the world their version of religion is attracting adherents in a way that few other religions are able to attract people—despite a theology that could, at best, be described as "strange."

But the Mormons, from the beginning, did not have a "professional" clergy. Instead—every member is considered a minister. Their young men and increasingly more young women, when they reach age eighteen, are sent overseas on a two-year mission to gain converts. The family finances these missions.

The Mormons currently have 44,000 full-time missionaries serving in 257 countries.

We who are Evangelical Lutheran Church in America members, who have depended on professionals to do the job, now have a total of 165 official, ordained missionaries! (But—here's the good news—that 165 only include the professionals. We as a church are reclaiming the calling of all God's people and now seventy percent of our ELCA missionaries are lay persons.)

Here is the reality: IF YOU ARE A DISCIPLE OF JESUS, YOU ARE CALLED INTO MINISTRY. That means several things for you:

First of all it means you must understand that you are called by God! God places you where you are and God depends only on you to accomplish that ministry!

Secondly, it means that you must DISCOVER your spiritual gifts and USE THEM in service to God and others. Jesus illustrated this so beautifully when he called his disciples. They were not learned men; they were common and some, like Levi, were even despised by others. Yet these twelve individuals turned the world upside down! They lived out the meaning of C.H.U.R.C.H.

Finally, if you are a disciple of Jesus, it means that you need to take mission more seriously.

We are Christ's hands and feet. We heal the sick, proclaim good news to the poor, feed the hungry and raise the dead. Jesus said, **"Very truly, I tell you, the one who believes in me will also do the works that I do and, in fact, will do greater works than these. . ."** (John 14:12)

As we CLAIM and USE our gifts, great, God-sized things will happen among us. Listen to what Jesus says in Matthew 11:28-30: **"Come to me, all you that are weary and are carrying heavy burdens, and I will give you rest. Take my yoke upon you, and learn from me; for I am gentle and humble in heart, and you will find rest for your souls. For my yoke is easy, and my burden is light."**

We all want and need to be used for a noble purpose. If Jesus can use people like Levi and Peter and James, he can surely use you and me!

A church often sees a great deal of self-centered behavior. But a C.H.U.R.C.H. that captures the creativity, energy, personality, education, experience, and presence of each individual's gifts, continually sees its joy rise and negativity diminish as participants quit treating church membership as some kind of privilege and start seeing membership as discipleship.

The real Super Bowl is being played out right here, right now—among us. This is the great drama. This is the great contest. This is where the action is. This is what it's all about.

That stuff we see on television: Super Bowls, Championship Playoffs, American Idol, Survivor—all are NOTHING compared to the incredible way God will use you and me in the days ahead.

More than forty years ago I heard a hymn on the radio that spoke to my heart in an unforgettable way:

Hark, the voice of Jesus calling, "Who will go and work today?
Fields are white and harvests waiting, Who will bear the sheaves away?
Loud and long the master calls you; Rich reward he offers free.
Who will answer gladly saying, "Here am I. Send me, send me"?

If you cannot speak like angels, If you cannot preach like Paul,
You can tell the love of Jesus; You can say he died for all.
If you cannot rouse the wicked With the judgment's dread alarms,
You can lead the little children To the Savior's waiting arms.

I especially like the fourth verse:

Let none hear you idly saying, "There is nothing I can do,"
While the multitudes are dying And the master calls for you.
Take the task he gives you gladly; Let his work your pleasure be.
Answer quickly when he calls you, "Here am I. Send me, send me!"

(Text: Daniel March, 1816-1909. Public domain)

No one of Christ's own can honestly say, "There is nothing I can do." Each of us has plenty to do. And when ministry is done, using the gifts and talents God has already given his people, then joy and satisfaction follow (to say nothing of the way the world is improved by the ministry, the service, performed).

The most difficult part of ministry, for most people, is not lacking the desire to serve, or even the time to serve. No, the most difficult part is the WHAT to do? In other words, HOW do I discover my gifts for ministry and then use them?

First, discovery: you can discover your gifts by simple prayer. Asking God to show you your gifts is a wonderful way to begin.

Where have you found great satisfaction? Maybe you had to substitute teach once and found that it was a wonderful experience and, dare you say it, you found joy in teaching. That satisfaction quotient is telling you that is at least one of your gifts.

Have others noticed something you have done in the past and commented on it? That also might be pointing to a spiritual gift.

What is your training? Are you a trained carpenter? That is a developed gift. Perhaps you are an accountant. Accounting would be another inclination that has been trained to perfection! What knowledge do you have that most others do not have? That may also point to a spiritual gift.

One way many churches seek to help people uncover their spiritual gifts is by a "Spiritual Gift Inventory." These are available from various sources: in print, on line, by subscription, etc. They can be useful but are probably less useful than simple prayer, self-insight, and the words of others that you have experienced in your life.

God has given us plenty to do and abundant gifts to do what needs to be done.

Our God is a God of great abundance. Only a few bushels of wheat are needed to plant a wheat field, but the field will produce thousands of bushels—all wheat that can be ground to flour and baked into bread. Similarly, God gives more than enough talents, gifts, abilities to an average church so that it can accomplish all God is calling it to do. Jesus told his disciples, **"The harvest is plentiful, but the laborers are few; therefore ask the Lord of the harvest to send out laborers into his harvest."** (Matthew 9:37b-38)

As a pastor I have seen far too many people who, with great good intentions, stepped in because the *organization* needed them and they had no gift for the calling.

I have seen too many good, Christian people, who, because no one else would teach, stepped forward to teach Sunday school and, in doing so, perhaps turned young lives away from the gospel instead of toward the good news. I have seen church members step forward to serve on church council because no one else would. Two years later they are so discouraged, they drop out of church. Too many times I have seen people step into roles outside their area of giftedness. I have seen far too many people ground down and chewed up by the church as an *organization* instead of uplifted by the church as a movement and calling.

God gives each congregation all the gifts it needs for its ministry. If suitable people cannot be found for a particular ministry, then that ministry needs to be ended. The principle should be PEOPLE FIRST; institution last.

Several years ago the Division for Congregational Ministries Stewardship and Mission Giving Team of the ELCA published a little book entitled THE GREAT PERMISSION. This little "Asset-Based Field Guide for Congregations" shows convincingly that congregations best use the assets they have and stop bemoaning what they do not have. The joy is knowing that we all have "assets"—gifts.

Here is a gold mine of tremendous personal satisfaction and joy as people hear the calling of God found in their giftedness and they respond to that calling with the answer: "Here am I send me, send me!"

LOOKING AT THE TEXTS

1. A little poem that's been around a long time goes, "How odd of God to choose the Jews." How does this saying play out in Jesus' choice of disciples?
2. How unlikely a choice are you? Do you feel deep down that sense of calling or is this a new idea for you? Discuss freely. *(We are all at a different place in our walk with Jesus).*
3. Discuss ways you have seen "professionals" like pastors hinder the utilization of God's gifted people.
4. What can a church do to help people discover their spiritual gifts? What can YOU do to discover YOUR gifts?
5. What can a church do to help people use their spiritual gifts? How will YOU use YOUR gifts?
6. Would you say church membership reflects discipleship or does it more closely resemble club membership with privileges?
7. How can the church more effectively cultivate discipleship and harvest the spiritual gifts of Christ's body? Discuss.

8. What will you do TODAY to discover and begin using your gifts? The Lord is saying to you: **"Whom shall I send, and who will go for us?"**

CHAPTER SIX

C.H.U.R.C.**H.** – **Hope**

MATTHEW 17:1-9

Six days later, Jesus took with him Peter and James and his brother John and led them up a high mountain, by themselves. And he was transfigured before them, and his face shone like the sun, and his clothes became dazzling white. Suddenly there appeared to them Moses and Elijah, talking with him. Then Peter said to Jesus, "Lord, it is good for us to be here; if you wish, I will make three dwellings here, one for you, one for Moses, and one for Elijah." While he was still speaking, suddenly a bright cloud overshadowed them, and from the cloud a voice said, "This is my Son, the Beloved; with him I am well pleased; listen to him!" When the disciples heard this, they fell to the ground and were overcome by fear. But Jesus came and touched them, saying, "Get up and do not be afraid." And when they looked up, they saw no one except Jesus himself alone.

ISAIAH 40:31

"Those who hope in the Lord will renew their strength. They will soar on wings like eagles; they will run and not grow weary, they will walk and not faint."

I have always thought it would be wonderful to have God speak to me directly. It would seem to clear up a great deal of ambiguity about religion. I can imagine myself asking God, "Why have you allowed so much suffering? Tell me, Lord, are we on the right path here as Lutherans or does someone else have faith practices that are more true to your intentions?" I can imagine asking, "Lord, just what is heaven all about? Can you be more specific?" I can see myself asking God, "Please tell me if I am serving you as you would have me serve you. Speak up if I get off track. Okay Lord?"

Many times in my life I have asked God to be more explicit. "Speak up, Lord." So often I have thought, "God, if only you would have spoken more directly I would have been more faithful." I have wanted to be a man of strong faith and bold witness, but when I ask for the voice of the Lord and get silence, that very silence tends to diminish my faith and lessens my passion for witness. I have never heard the voice of the Lord directly. But I believe it can happen and does happen. After all, it happened to Jesus didn't it?

When I was a child, I fantasized that the pastor spoke directly to the Lord. Sometimes I wonder if this fantasy, this personal hope, helped propel me into the ordained ministry? (Maybe God will personally speak to me?) In our little country church the chancel area had two doors. I had never seen the lectern-side door opened. My imagination told me that is where the pastor went to get inspiration for his sermons and that is where the ushers took the money to give to God. In reality I now suspect the door led to a storage closet.

Sometimes popular television shows such as "Touched by an Angel" and "Joan of Arcadia" or movies such as that old classic, "It's a Wonderful Life" played out my childhood fantasies. In these shows and some popular movies, God or an agent of God speaks clearly and directly.

In the Bible there are only two occasions where God speaks directly even to Jesus: One, right after his baptism and before his temptation in the wilderness; the other is the reading for TRANSFIGURATION—a time right before Jesus' journey to Jerusalem where he would suffer horribly and die.

Notice the timing of God's voice—right before terrible stresses and strains on Jesus' own life:

First Jesus is baptized. It is a wonderful time of celebration and the voice of God. **"Now when all the people were baptized, and when Jesus also had been baptized and was praying, the heaven was opened, and the Holy Spirit descended upon him in bodily form like a dove. And a voice came from heaven, 'You are my Son,**

the Beloved; with you I am well pleased.'" (Luke 3:21-22) Then comes the Temptation: forty days of fasting, loneliness, isolation. But how grand it must have been to see the heaven opened and the Holy Spirit descending. And then to hear the voice. . . Except for the fact that it was in the Jordan River, it must have been a "mountain top" experience for those who saw and heard—especially for Jesus. It was confirmation for him. Or, as we Lutherans say today, "Affirmation of Baptism."

The second time in the Bible where we hear of God speaking to Jesus is the Transfiguration: **"suddenly a bright cloud overshadowed them, and from the cloud a voice said, 'This is my Son, the Beloved; with him I am well pleased; listen to him!'"** (Matthew 17:5)

I have spoken to people who believe they have heard God's voice in their lives. Some share a spiritual vision. I remember, for example, a woman named Bertha Staley who was our organist at the first church I served in Kansas. One evening at a Bible study in one of the member's homes, she shared this story:

"When I was a little girl, my sister and I were in bed together. Momma was very sick. I hadn't gone to sleep yet, but my sister had. Then, suddenly, from the side of the room, a figured walked to the end of our bed, looked down on us, turned and walked away—disappearing into the wall without saying a word.

"I woke my sister up and got out of bed, threw aside the rug at the foot of our bed and took a piece of chalk and put an 'X' at the spot where the figure stood. I put the rug back over the spot and went back to bed.

"Shortly after that, our father came up to our room and took us in his arms and said, 'Mommy has died.'

"I have believed all these years that what I saw was an angel."

I have no doubt that is what Bertha saw. Her story simply has too much detail to be a fantasy, dream, or the magical thinking of a child who has now grown up. Others have told me similar stories of clearly hearing a voice or seeing an angel or even seeing Jesus himself. I have had several experiences of calling on people who were in the last stages of life and yet report vivid "dreams" where Jesus spoke or a loved one shared words of comfort. But, interestingly, whenever there was a voice or vision, it has come before some traumatic, stress-filled, painful and horrific event or drama.

As I've thought about it, I'm not so sure I really do want to hear God's voice. In fact I KNOW I wouldn't want to hear God's voice. It would scare the daylights out of me. I would wonder what's coming next. What bad thing is going to happen to me?

Without hearing God's voice directly, I've got only one means of believing in God: FAITH. Faith cannot be proven by science, reason or experiential proof. It is, as scripture says, a gift. As a gift it cannot be earned—it can only be received or rejected.

A by-product of faith is hope. I like the story of Florence Chadwick who was the first woman to swim the English Channel both ways. She didn't quite make it on her first attempt. It wasn't the cold water. It wasn't the sharks. It wasn't the 15-hour swim. It was the fact that the fog rolled in and she couldn't see the coastline. She quit half a mile from the goal. When she got out of the water she said, "I'm not trying to make an excuse but I feel like if the fog hadn't been there and I could have seen the land, I would have made it." Later she tried again. The fog rolled in again but this time she knew that the coastline was there. And she completed the journey. In fact, she did it in two fewer hours than anybody else had ever done it.

It was her faith in the shore being there that gave her hope. Sight couldn't do it. Only faith.

When FAITH is present, I have hope.

FAITH is a gift of God. HOPE is a gift of FAITH.

Faith and hope go together. And what happens when we have hope? There are several practical results of a hope-filled life.

One practical result is that I can endure.

Isaiah 40:31 reminds us that, **"Those who hope in the Lord will renew their strength. They will soar on wings like eagles; they will run and not grow weary, they will walk and not faint."**

If I can endure, then I can live with…. Fill in the blank. What can you live with because of hope in your life? You can live with…

whatever burden is in your life right now. You can make it through. It is hope that enables us to handle tremendous pressure.

People who have hope can handle incredible amounts of burden in their lives.

Hopeful people are like the apostle Paul, in 2 Corinthians 1:8, when talking about the burdens that he had because of the persecution that he faced: **"We had great burdens that were beyond our own strength. We even gave up the hope of living."** [Perhaps you feel that way today as you read these words?] **But this happened so we would trust not in ourselves but in God."** Even at that point where he wondered, "Am I going to make it?" he was able to find hope. He could live with anything because of the hope that God gave him—and so can we. Hope is a wonderful by-product of faith.

A second result of hope is the knowledge that I can go on. Hope is what gives us the strength to go on after a loss or a disappointment or a dream that refuses to become reality.

Like Florence Chadwick attempting to swim the English Channel The fog has rolled into our lives and we've lost our bearings. Like a coastline, God's promises are immovable even if we can't see them. They're going to be there. Hope is out there in the future. That's what hope does in our lives.

I like this verse about hope in 1 Peter 1:6 from the Living Bible, **"So be truly glad! There is wonderful joy ahead, even though the going is rough for a while down here."** When I have hope I can live with anything, and I can go on.

Thirdly, hope gives me the power to say no. I can endure anything, I can go on, and I can say no to the temptations of life. Hope is the foundation of integrity. If I have no hope for the future, then truthfully there is no logical reason to live a life of integrity.

1 John 3:3 says, **"Everyone who has this hope in Christ keeps himself pure just as Christ is pure."** That's the power of hope in our lives—it keeps us pure and motivates us to holy living.

Hope is the missing ingredient in many peoples' lives. When troubles come, they are devastated. When disappointments show up on the doorstep, many people invite them in the house. Since there is no lasting hope, character development and lives of integrity are not even on the horizon.

Hope is an outcome of FAITH. Faith is a gift of God. God uses the C.H.U.R.C.H. for FAITH and HOPE development.

Hope trusts in God and knows God provides.

I recently read a story about a man who walked out of a beautiful cathedral in one of our large, American cities on Easter Monday. The day was a splendid spring day and the man had a sense of peace deep down. He met a woman selling flowers and noticed how happy she was. "You certainly look happy," he said.

"Oh yes. Why not?" she answered. "Everything is good."

Yet her clothes were shabby and she seemed so wrinkled and old that the woman's reply startled the man.

"Every time I see you you are always smiling," he said to her.

"I've seen my share of trouble," the woman said. "But when trouble comes I think of Jesus and Good Friday. Good Friday was the worst day in the world, but in just three days, it was Easter Sunday— the best day in the world."

"When troubles come to me," she said, "I've learned to wait three days. And every time, those troubles faded in just three short days. I've learned to wait."

The secret behind this woman's joy was revealed. Her simple faith, coupled with hope, brought a face with smiles.

So again, we see that HOPE is a by-product of FAITH.

In my own life I have had times of tremendous stress. When in those times of stress, my human nature told me to be afraid and to go ahead and despair. But my faith told me to trust God and that some day this would all pass and I would learn valuable lessons from this time of trial.

That has been the case with EVERY trial and circumstance. God pulls me through whatever I must endure.

Who teaches FAITH?

Will you find television producers giving us inspirational stories of faith? Usually not. (More likely, we'll have stories of murder, treachery, lying and deceit). Will the business world teach us that faith is more important than anything else? (I don't think so!). Will schools teach us about faith and prayer and hope? (They won't—even though many people wish they would).

I have a close relative who strongly believes there should be prayer in the schools of our land, but she never bothered to consistently attend church or have prayer in her home while her children were growing up. Like her, they also believe in prayer in the schools, but don't practice it at home. The church has to be supported by parents if children are going to learn true hope. Real faith is learned at home and at church—not at school.

Who will teach us about FAITH and HOPE? Is there any HOPE of learning about real, substantial HOPE? It is obvious and self evident that the only substantive teaching about faith and hope must come from the C.H.U.R.C.H.! We are, after all, a HOPE movement; a process; a daily event and a relationship. We are much less an institution.

I am passionate about the C.H.U.R.C.H. because it gives people what we all need. I have no doubt that the very HOPE of the world is in those communities of faith that live out God's vision of C.H.U.R.C.H.

Let's review what that means:

C=Christ. He is at the center of all that we are and do. Nothing takes his place. In him we have our faith and trust. He has shown us how to have hope that is out of this world!

H=Home. The church is a safe place where we are accepted as we are. It is a place we can truly be ourselves and where we can share our sorrows as well as our hopes and dreams.

U=Urgency. This good news just can't wait. We've GOT to get the Word out!

R=Relationships. There is that all-important relationship between ourselves and our God. Then there are the relationships between ourselves and others. We need other people. We need to know and be known.

C=Calling. We are called into ministry by baptism. It is a holy and an awesome calling. But it is also incredibly thrilling to live out our calling in faith.

H=Hope.

The C.H.U.R.C.H. teaches FAITH which leads to HOPE which leads to FULLNESS OF LIFE.

I liked it the Sunday everyone stood up and faced outward—toward one of the four walls of the church building. Having everyone fact OUTWARD from the church was, to me, a dramatic symbol of what we are called to do: look and reach outward. The church is a movement and so much more than a building and an exercise like this highlights that fact.

Think of it this way: since you are the church, you are a HOPE-bearer. I am a HOPE-bearer. There are thousands of people out there beyond the church walls. You probably can't see them now, but they are there. They are looking for something to believe in. They are looking for something that is real. They are looking for answers that satisfy their deepest longings. And God is depending on YOU and ME to get the word to them because WE ARE THE CHURCH.

To be a G.O.O.D. church, we have to "Get Outside Our Doors"

I love the Benediction from Romans 15:13 so let us close this book with it: **"Now may the God of hope fill you with great joy and peace as you trust in him, so that you may overflow with hope by the power of the Holy Spirit."**

LOOKING AT THE TEXTS

1. Have you ever experienced a vision or the voice of Jesus in your life? *(Please do not be embarrassed to share)*. If so, why do you think this experience happened to you?
2. What would be your response to the person who says, "There is no God because I cannot see, hear, touch, or experience God"?

3. Why do you think God so often chooses to remain silent (especially in the face of suffering and tragedy)?

4. Is faith something we choose or something we can prove in one way or another? (Or, is faith something else entirely?)

5. Can hope spring from something other than faith? If so, what?

6. The American Skeptic Robert G. Ingersoll said, "I suppose it can be truthfully said that Hope is the only universal liar who never loses his reputation for veracity." What do you suppose he meant and how would you answer?

7. On a scale of 1 (= highest) to 10 (= lowest), how effective is the church as a community of HOPE in this world? How could our effectiveness improve?

To Summarize C.H.U.R.C.H.:

1) Always seek to keep "the main thing the main thing": **CHRIST.** (It is easy to get off track!)

2) Ministry best takes place at **HOME:**

   a) Where parents and children live out the baptismal promises to: *"live with them among God's faithful people, bring them to the word of God and the holy supper, teach them. . . place in their hands the holy scriptures, and nurture them in faith and prayer, so that your children may learn to trust God, proclaim Christ. . . care for others and the world God made. . . " (Evangelical Lutheran Worship, p. 228)*

   b) The church is a safe place for all people where we are loved "as is" and where each person is profoundly respected and honored and judgment is left to God.

3) The Good News is **URGENTLY** needed in the world and we seek to grow in our ability to share this good news with family, friends, and co-workers in ways that are natural and genuine.

4) **RELATIONSHIPS** grow to deeper levels by the deliberate drive to create new small groups where people can know and be known and grow spiritually in relationship with God and one another.

5) Knowing that we are **CALLED** into ministry, we know and understand our unique giftedness and use those gifts to serve God and others.
   a) We develop and use tools such as gifts inventories, personal feedback, and a high "satisfaction quotient" (as well as "time and talent" forms) for self understanding.
   b) We step forward with a desire to serve eagerly and enthusiastically by using our gifts for ministry.
6) Spread **HOPE** wherever we are and understand that God has called each of us, as the C.H.U.R.C.H. to be HOPE bearers and HOPE-filled people.

Printed in the United States
123598LV00003B/583-678/P

9 780595 528455